Political Change and Industrial
Development in Japan: .
Government Enterprise, 1868-1880

WHEN WESTERN INFLUENCE reached Asia in new force through channels of trade in the middle of the nineteenth century, the responses of China and Japan were startlingly different. For China, the Western impact meant the eventual collapse of her traditional society; for Japan, new strength through a transition from an almost purely agrarian to a predominantly industrial economy. This radical transition was achieved by a forced march to industrialization, triggered by a political revolution. It is the critical phase of that forced march, when government enterprise was dominant, that Dr. Smith examines and interprets in this study.

Thomas C. Smith is an associate professor of history at Stanford University. His bachelor's degree is from Santa Barbara College and his doctorate from Harvard University. During World War II he was a Japanese language officer with the U.S. Marine Corps, and during the postwar period he served in the same capacity with the occupation forces in Japan.

Political Change and Industrial
Development in Japan:
Government Enterprise, 1868-1880

By

THOMAS C. SMITH

STANFORD UNIVERSITY PRESS, STANFORD, CALIFORNIA

LONDON: GEOFFREY CUMBERLEGE, OXFORD UNIVERSITY PRESS

1955

Stanford University Publications
University Series

History, Economics, and Political Science
Volume X

STANFORD UNIVERSITY PRESS, STANFORD, CALIFORNIA

PUBLISHED IN GREAT BRITAIN AND INDIA BY GEOFFREY CUMBERLEGE,
OXFORD UNIVERSITY PRESS, LONDON AND BOMBAY

HENRY M. SNYDER & COMPANY, INC., 440 FOURTH AVENUE, NEW YORK 16
W. S. HALL & COMPANY, 510 MADISON AVENUE, NEW YORK 22

Library of Congress Catalog Card Number: 55-6687

Preface

WHOEVER makes the comparison cannot fail to note the sharply different responses of China and Japan to the intrusion of the West. To state the difference oversimply: traditional Chinese society after a prolonged agony of resistance to alien influences collapsed, opening the way to drastic change, while Japanese society adapted, changing more rapidly but in important respects less radically as a result.

The disruptive wedge of Western influence in Asia was trade, to which both China and Japan were opened wide by commercial treaties thrust on them by superior force in the middle of the nineteenth century. In both cases the initial economic consequences were approximately the same: a flood of machine-made goods progressively destroyed indigenous handicraft industry whose products were simpler, cruder, and for the most part dearer. This has been noted by many writers, but it has not been sufficiently stressed. What was destroyed was not merely the living of a small artisan class, but the margin that permitted the peasant to farm successfully. For, both in China and Japan, except for crafts that by their refinement were arts, handicraft industry was an adjunct to agriculture and was carried on in peasant homes.

In China this destructive process continued with nothing emerging to replace what the peasant economy lost. As a consequence, not only was the equilibrium of agriculture upset and the peasantry driven to rebellion and finally to revolution; the vitality of Chinese institutions was smothered at the source. When, in the twentieth century, China's leaders first awoke fully to China's plight, decline had gone too far for recovery built on the inheritance of the past. Grandiose plans for restoring life to expiring institutions were endlessly spun, but so enfeebled was the state, so parlous the treasury, and so shaken the leaders that men with the best of intentions were powerless to carry plans beyond the precincts of government bureaus. So the loss of strength continued in the old way despite the wish to reform, until frustration and despair created new forces of awful violence and power that would reconstruct Chinese society along revolutionary lines.

Japan started down the same steep road to national disaster, but saved herself midway by something like a forced march to industrialization that began with a political revolution. The speed of the march was important, since a new economic base for political power had to be created before the traditional one, already violently shaken, gave way—unless there was to be a long intermediate period of foreign encroachment and national impotence during which almost everything traditionally Japanese would become a symbol of failure. Instead, within a generation of the revolution of 1868, the transition from an almost purely agrarian to a predominantly in-

v

dustrial economy had been made; and by the strength this transition developed, Japan was not only made safe from the encroachment of expansive Western powers, she was enabled to join them and pick up imperialist prizes that brought additional strength. Equally important, since old values sanctioned the innovations and the wrenching and painful adjustments these entailed, Japan's past was looked upon as the ultimate source of her strength and so became part of her future.

Although from time to time for contrast we will touch upon events in China, this book is concerned with Japan, during what might be called the critical phase of the forced march—from 1868 to 1880, when government enterprise was dominant. This was the most critical period of Japanese industrialization for two reasons: first, because industrialization, so far as history yet records, is more difficult to initiate than sustain; and, second, because initial failure or even delay would have been fatal, as it proved in China. These early years, then, should throw more light than later periods on how the Japanese feat of industrialization, unique in Asia to the middle of the twentieth century, was accomplished. This is the general question that concerns us, but it must be broken into more specific and manageable parts. One cannot treat everything relevant to so radical a development as industrialization because in one way or another almost everything is relevant, and twelve years are a long time when things are happening fast. Our particular questions, which we will ask as we go along, are by no means the only relevant ones and we cannot claim that together they elicit a complete answer to the general question with which we start. It will be enough if they are significant questions and the answers to them cast light in occasional dark corners. There is another limitation to be mentioned here: no attempt has been made to deal with the industrial development of Hokkaidō, since the basic collection of materials on the economic history of our period does not cover that island.

I wish to record my thanks to Professors Edwin O. Reischauer and John K. Fairbank, under whose direction at Harvard this was originally written as a doctoral dissertation; to Professor Serge Elisseeff for friendly advice and encouragement; to Professor Nobutaka Ike who read the entire manuscript; to Mr. Kaiming Ch'iu for solicitous help when I was learning to find my way around the Japanese collection at Harvard; to Mrs. Barbara de Kins and Mrs. Jeanne Smith who helped edit the manuscript. Finally, I wish to thank the Stanford University Press for making possible publication of this book.

THOMAS C. SMITH

PALO ALTO, CALIFORNIA
June 1954

Contents

Abbreviations

Kzgrs	*Keizai gaku ronshū* (*Journal of Economics*)
Kzrs	*Keizai ronsō* (*Journal of Economics*)
Kzskk	*Keizai shi kenkyū* (*Studies in Economic History*)
Mzks	*Meiji zaisei keizai shiryō shūsei* (*Materials on Economics and Finance in the Meiji Period*)
Kzsj	*Nihon keizai shi jiten* (*Dictionary of Japanese Economic History*)
Zskzsr	*Nihon zaisei keizai shiryō* (*Materials on Japanese Economy and Finance*)
Rgk	*Rekishi gaku kenkyū* (*Historical Studies*)
Sks	*Shakai keizai shigaku* (*Social and Economic History*)
Sz	*Shigaku zasshi* (*Journal of History*)

I. The Beginnings of Modern Industry

THE MODERN period of Japanese history is usually dated from 1868, the year of the Meiji Restoration. Like most dates used in defining historical periods, this one gives the illusion of a sharp break in historical development that did not occur in fact, for many distinctive characteristics of modern Japan may be clearly traced at least as far back as the late Tokugawa period. Even so recent a feature as industrialization began in the closing years of the "feudal" period with the introduction of Western technology and methods in several branches of industry. It is the purpose of this chapter to describe the conditions under which this movement began, suggest the scope and character of the process, and attempt to estimate its significance for the industrial history of the Meiji period.

I

Industrialization began earlier and proceeded more rapidly in Japan than elsewhere in the Far East. One of the reasons for this was that knowledge of the West, and particularly its technology, was more advanced in Japan than elsewhere almost from the beginning of Western intercourse. This is the more remarkable because, after a period of nearly free intercourse, the Tokugawa cut Japan off from all direct contact with Europe, except for a very limited trade with the Dutch at Nagasaki, in the early part of the seventeenth century—just on the eve of those great scientific achievements in Europe that led indirectly to machine industry. There seems no satisfactory way of accounting for Japan's continuing intellectual interest in the West, despite isolation. Perhaps we can do no better than remark what seems to be a strong native Japanese curiosity and to add that isolation appears to have intensified rather than dulled it. Whatever the explanation, a restless desire for knowledge of the outside world drove increasing numbers of Japanese throughout the Tokugawa period to attempt to learn Dutch; at first in the face of strong official disapproval and almost without hope of success, for there were no dictionaries, no grammars, no competent teachers until well into the eighteenth century. Needless to say, little progress was made during the first century of Dutch studies, but neither was the period wholly barren of results. Out of the incredibly painful labors of a handful of men there gradually emerged something like comprehension of the structure of the Dutch language and an intimation of the riches locked up in Dutch books.[1]

Toward the end of the eighteenth century practical results came with a

---

[1] C. R. Boxer, *Jan Companie in Japan, 1600–1817* (The Hague, 1936), chaps. 3, 4. Donald Keene, *The Japanese Discovery of Europe: Honda Toshiaki and Other Discoverers, 1720–1789* (London, 1952), pp. 21–29.

1

rush. Within a few decades grammars were written, dictionaries compiled, private language schools founded, the practice of "Dutch medicine" developed into an established profession, and scores of books or parts of books translated from the Dutch on a wide range of subjects—geography, anatomy, medicine, astronomy, military science, shipbuilding, explosives, chemistry, history, and politics, to mention but a few. And from these translations knowledge and appreciation of the Western world spread beyond the little corps of "Dutch scholars" to men who themselves knew no Dutch. The sudden blossoming of Dutch studies was not merely a result of increasing mastery of the language; this would leave unexplained the general quickening of interest in Dutch studies. To explain the new interest at all adequately we must note the growing dissatisfaction in Japan during the eighteenth century—particularly dissatisfaction among the *samurai*, or warriors, whose economic position was deteriorating as a result of a powerfully developing money economy. Dutch studies provided material that lent authenticity to idealized constructions of happier societies half a world away, the contemplation of which was a substitute for protest the political system suppressed.[2] Dutch studies also provided material for clandestine or indirect criticism of the regime. Much as Voltaire used the example of China to criticize the French monarchy and the church, Satō Nobuhiro used the history of the maritime nations of the West, especially England, to demonstrate the fatuousness of Tokugawa economic and military policies.[3] But criticism and escape were not the only values of Dutch studies: they had strategic value as well, and for this reason the Tokugawa dared not suppress them despite their clearly subversive tendency.

The growing crisis in Japan's foreign relations from the late eighteenth century on made Dutch studies part of a program of national defense. No one doubted, or confessed to doubt, that the Japanese were essentially— that is, "spiritually"—superior to the people who menaced them, but nearly everyone conceded the superiority of Western technology.[4] "It is astonishing," Sakuma Shonan exclaimed, "that, with the invention of the steamship, the magnet, and the telegraph, they [Westerners] now appear to control the laws of nature."[5] Such opinion was not a counsel of despair: "Western technology" could be put at the service of "Japanese spirit" and Dutch studies would show how. They would also reveal the secret motivations and intentions of Western man—a knowledge that would permit the Japanese to check and control him. "To defend ourselves against the barbarians," a Mito offi-

---

[2] An illustration of this tendency is Ando Shoeki, perhaps the severest Tokugawa critic of Japanese society. See Ando's remarks in praise of Holland, quoted in Maruyama Masao, *Nihon seiji shisō shi kenkyū* (*Studies in Japanese Political Thought*) (Tokyo, 1952), p. 265.

[3] Takimoto Seiichi (ed.), *Satō Nobuhiro kegaku zenshū* (*Works of the Family of Satō Nobuhiro*) (Tokyo, 1927), III, 757–831.

[4] For example, see the *Shinron* of the Mito scholar, Aizawa Yasashi; edited by Takasu Yoshijiro (Tokyo, 1941), pp. 13–77.

[5] Quoted in Honjō Eijirō, "A Survey of Economic Thought in the Closing Days of the Tokugawa Period," *Kyoto University Economic Review*, XIII (Oct. 1938), 25.

cial wrote, "we must know them and ourselves: the way to know them is through Dutch studies."[6]

Only the Tokugawa and some of the large *han*[7]—Satsuma, Chōshū, Saga, Tosa, and Mito—had the resources to promote Dutch studies, but together they accomplished much. Each established an official school to teach *samurai* the Dutch language and to give instruction in various branches of "Dutch learning." Most of these schools were established before Perry's arrival in Japan, and some had surprisingly varied curricula. For example, the Tokugawa school, which was known as the "Place for the Study of Barbarian Books" (*Bansho shirabesho*), taught Western mathematics, astronomy, geography, physics, metallurgy, and by 1866 offered instruction in English, German, French, and Russian in addition to Dutch. Associated with most of these schools, and in some cases antedating them, were official translation bureaus that did important work. The translation bureau of the Tokugawa government, where some of the most famous Dutch scholars of the time were employed, dated from 1808, possibly earlier, and turned out translations on such subjects as medicine, chemistry, mechanics, and mining, as well as a translation of an encyclopedia that ran to seventy volumes and required twenty-eight years to complete. At least two of the *han*, Satsuma and Saga, in addition to schools, founded laboratories to experiment with the practical applications of "Dutch learning"—photography, cotton spinning, sugar refining, the plating of metals, and the manufacture of acids, alcohol, and glass. These laboratories also built for experimental purposes models of the reverberatory furnace, the steamship, and the telegraph.[8]

We may doubt that before Perry's arrival there was anything like a firm theoretical understanding of any of the subjects studied and, except for the Dutch language itself, even practical mastery. But this was relatively unimportant: enough was known to convince not only Dutch scholars but officials generally of the potentialities of modern technology, and there was a hard-won body of empirical data on which to build genuine understanding. By 1850 Japan had gone through an apprenticeship that lay almost entirely in the future for China. And it was at least partly for this reason that Japan

---

[6] Tokugawa kōshaku ke (ed.), *Mito han shiryō* (*Historical Materials on the Mito Han*) (Tokyo, 1916), I, 919.

[7] The territory under the jurisdiction of a Tokugawa vassal of the first rank (*daimyō*) was called a *han*. This term is usually translated as "fief" or "clan," but neither term is a happy rendering and I have chosen to use the Japanese term throughout.

[8] Numata Jirō, "Bansho shirabesho ni tsuite" ("Concerning . . . the Place for the Study of Barbarian Books"), *Rekishi chiri* (*History and Geography*), LXXI (May 1938), 18–19, 24, 29–31. Ōkurashō (ed.), *Zskzsr* (Tokyo, 1922–25), X, 960. Horie Yasuzō, "Yamaguchi han ni okeru bakumatsu no yōshiki kōgyō" ("Western Industry in the Yamaguchi *Han* at the End of the Tokugawa Period"), *Kzrs*, XL (Jan. 1935), 155, 164, and "Nakajima Jihei to Yamaguchi han no yōshiki kōgyō" ("Nakajima Jihei and Western Industry in the Yamaguchi *Han*"), *Kzrs*, XL (May 1935), 135–37. *Mito han shiryō*, I, 916, 919, 921. Etō Tsuneharu, "Bakumatsu ni okeru Kōchi han no shinseisaku" ("The New Policy of the Kōchi *Han* in the Late Tokugawa Period"), *Kzskk*, XIV (Sept. 1935), 1–4, 12. Tsuchiya Takao, *Hōken shakai hōkai katei no kenkyū* (*A Study of the Disintegration of Feudal Society*) (Tokyo, 1927), pp. 489–91, 512–13, 527–29.

had greater success in the critical years between 1850 and 1880 in applying the new technology, as the early history of modern industry in Japan suggests.

II

Once the military potentialities of modern technology were grasped, it was a short step to attempt to develop the industries necessary to realizing them. That the Tokugawa and the leading *han*, upon whom the burden of national defense principally fell, were acting under what they interpreted as military pressure affected the early history of modern industry in Japan in two important respects. First, the earliest and most important industries developed during the Tokugawa period, such as iron, armaments, and ship-building, were strategic in character. Second, the urgency of developing the new industries and the absence of a capitalist class with traditions and experience in industrial undertakings precluded their development being left to private interests.

Saga was the first *han* to introduce modern methods of smelting iron ore, a fact closely related to Saga's defensive assignment and to the relatively advanced state of Dutch studies in Saga. Since the seventeenth century Saga had been charged with responsibility for the defense of Nagasaki in alternate years with the Fukuoka *han*. The inadequacy of existing defensive works became increasingly evident during the first part of the nineteenth century, and in 1850 Saga drew up a plan for strengthening the port's defenses by emplacing a total of fifty-three guns, varying in size from twelve to one hundred and fifty pounds, on the islands lying immediately off the coast. At that time weapons were cast almost exclusively from copper because the traditional methods of smelting iron ore did not yield high-quality iron in sufficient quantity for the purpose. As guns were cast in increasing numbers in the first half of the century, copper became prohibitively expensive and difficult to procure. Confronted with the necessity of using iron to carry out its defensive plan and consequently of finding a more efficient means of smelting the ore, Saga, in 1850, three years before Perry's arrival, built the first successful reverberatory furnace in Japan, using a Dutch book as guide.[9]

The capacity of this furnace soon proved inadequate, and three additional furnaces were built in quick succession.[10] The success of the undertaking was confirmed in 1853 when an iron gun was satisfactorily cast from one of the new furnaces. Sugitani Yasusuke, the translator of the book used in building the furnaces, expressed in his diary satisfaction with the results. "Even though this gun is not the equal of those made in the West," he wrote, "the difference is not very great."[11] The *daimyō* of Saga must have shared Sugi-

---

[9] Etō Tsuneharu, "Takashima tankō ni okeru kyūhan makki no Nichiei kyōdō kigyō ("The Joint Anglo-Japanese Coal-Mining Enterprise at Takashima in the Late Tokugawa Period"), *Kzskk*, XIII (Feb. 1935), 37–39, 46. *Mito han shiryō*, I, 345, 352. Horie, "Yamaguchi han," p. 153.

[10] Etō, "Takashima tankō," p. 48.

[11] Quoted in Ōyama Futarō, "Bakumatsu ni okeru yōshiki seitetsu jigyō" ("Western-Style Iron Industry in the Late Tokugawa Period"), *Kzskk*, XX (Aug. 1938), 16.

tani's opinion because Saga cast guns from iron on a considerable scale after 1853. We have no figures on output, but about one hundred workers were employed in casting during the first three years of the enterprise, and Saga filled an order from the Tokugawa for two hundred of the new guns before 1857.[12]

Other *han* as well as the Tokugawa government watched the progress of the Saga experiment with keen interest, for they were likewise compelled by the increasing pressure of foreign powers to expand their armaments. Satsuma, Mito, and the Tokugawa quickly followed the example of Saga, and by 1858 all three had succeeded in building one or more reverberatory furnaces. Other *han* were less successful: Chōshū began a furnace but failed to complete it,[13] and Tosa, Jōshū, Tottori, and Kuroda never got beyond the planning stage. Why these efforts failed is not clear, but the case of Tosa, which found a furnace too expensive, suggests that financial difficulties were a common cause.[14]

Even before the success of the Saga furnace had been ascertained, Satsuma built a model furnace, using Sugitani's translation. Experiments in the smelting of ore were made with the model, and in 1853 Satsuma built a full-sized reverberatory furnace and a blast furnace the following year. Two additional furnaces of the reverberatory type were built in 1865. In the same year Satsuma built from sketches in a Dutch book a *sankaidai*, a device powered by a water wheel for boring the solid iron barrels cast from the furnaces.[15]

The iron produced with these furnaces was used chiefly for casting weapons, and a lively armaments industry developed at Kagoshima, the seat of government in Satsuma. Shimazu Nariakira, the energetic *daimyō* of Satsuma, also established a number of small workshops to produce for sale a variety of iron products such as carpentry tools and agricultural implements. The iron and armaments industry, together with these workshops and a number of others for sugar refining and for the manufacture of leather articles and paper, was collectively known as the *Shūseikan*. Although there are no data on output of iron by Satsuma, the fact that twelve hundred workers were being employed at the *Shūseikan* in 1858 is suggestive of the size and importance of the iron industry there.[16]

The origin of the iron industry in Mito was similar to that of Satsuma and Saga in that the necessity of casting guns from iron led to the construction of Western-style furnaces for smelting ore.[17] There are, however, a number of details of the Mito industry that have special interest. They indicate a sur-

[12] *Ibid.*, pp. 16–17. Etō, "Takashima tankō," p. 49.

[13] Chōshū began construction of a furnace from sketches of the Saga furnace made by a Chōshū official; work on the furnace was abandoned because of the expense of the undertaking and the fact that Chōshū officials came to regard the guns cast by Saga as unsatisfactory. Horie, "Yamaguchi han," p. 161.

[14] Ōyama, "Yōshiki seitetsu jigyō," p. 23. Etō, "Kōchi han no shinseisaku," p. 20.

[15] Tsuchiya, *Hōken shakai hōkai*, pp. 491–94.

[16] *Ibid.*, pp. 491, 498. Horie Yasuzō, "Bakumatsu no gunji kōgyō" ("Military Industry in the Late Tokugawa Period"), *Kzskk*, XIX (May 1938), 4.

[17] *Mito han shiryō*, I, 345.

prising degree of co-operation among particular *han* and throw some light on the financial problems raised by establishment of the new enterprises.

Co-operation with other *han* antedated the introduction of modern industry by Mito. Tokugawa Nariaki, the Lord of Mito, had earlier exchanged Dutch books with other *daimyō*, and in 1851 Mito was permitted to send a representative to Satsuma and Saga to inspect the work being done by these *han* on the reverberatory furnace. Two years later, when Satsuma had at last succeeded in smelting ore, Shimazu Nariakira of Satsuma reported the event to the Lord of Mito in considerable detail.[18] By this time, however, Mito had already embarked on a similar project. Mito had obtained the services of Ōshima Takatō, a *samurai* of the Nambu *han* who had been studying the reverberatory furnace from Dutch books, and Takeshita Norimichi, a Satsuma *samurai* who had worked on the furnace at Kagoshima.[19] By 1853 these outsiders had produced a model furnace for Mito and the construction of a full-sized furnace had been ordered.[20]

Construction of one of the new furnaces entailed a substantial outlay. Mito was unable to finance the project entirely from its own treasury and was obliged to ask for a loan of 10,000 *ryō* from the Tokugawa. In April of 1854 the Tokugawa granted the loan and acceded to the proposed condition that the loan be repaid in weapons cast after the furnace was completed. Construction was begun four months later under the technical direction of Ōshima and Takeshita, and the furnace was completed in December 1855, after little more than twelve months' work. A second furnace was begun several months later and finished in June 1856. A *sankaidai* had already been completed in 1855, and a blast furnace was built in 1858, marking the completion of the Mito iron industry.[21]

Despite the fact that the Tokugawa bore the primary responsibility for national defense, it was not until 1858 that the Tokugawa government built a reverberatory furnace. Even then, the initiative came from an extraordinary Tokugawa provincial official, Egawa Tarōzaemon, who had built a small but unsuccessful furnace as early as 1842 at Nirayama in Izu Province.[22] Egawa dispatched a subordinate to study the Saga furnace, and, stimulated by news of its success, requested permission from his superiors in Edo to build a second furnace in his district. Permission was granted and after several years' labor the furnace was completed at Nirayama and the casting of guns was begun in 1858, three years after Egawa's death.[23]

After 1858 the Tokugawa developed the iron industry in connection with

---

[18] Tsuchiya, *op. cit.*, p. 492. Ōyama, "Yōshiki seitetsu jigyō," p. 19.

[19] *Mito han shiryō*, I, 344, 919.

[20] *Ibid.*, p. 344.

[21] *Ibid.*, pp. 345, 348, 350–52. Ōyama, "Yōshiki seitetsu jigyō," p. 22

[22] *Ibid.*, p. 14. Egawa was *daikan* (a local administrative official) of the Kamo district in Izu Province. He was one of the most progressive men of his day: he was a student of Dutch, advocated the use of commoners as soldiers, and studied European artillery, mathematics, and surveying.

[23] *Zskzsr*, I, 1000.

shipbuilding. The two industries are so intimately related in the materials for their study as well as in fact, it will be convenient to consider them together.

III

Since the year 1635 the Tokugawa, as part of a program for eliminating factors of growth and change that might disturb their dominance, had prohibited the construction of seagoing vessels. It was not until 1853, when the arrival of Perry gave new evidence of the danger to the nation from foreign powers, that the prohibition was lifted to make possible the building of a navy. There is no doubt of the motivation behind this abandonment of a policy vital to the perpetuation of Tokugawa rule. It was to national defense that the Lord of Mito appealed in petitioning for a reversal of policy as early as the Tempō era (1830–44), and the language of the decree announcing the new policy in 1853 permitted the construction of large ships (*taisen*) "because in the present state of affairs, they are necessary. . . ." A supplementary decree spoke of ships as "necessary for maritime defense."[24] Thus, the immediate stimulus for the introduction of modern shipbuilding, which dates from this measure, clearly came from the menace of foreign aggression.

The Tokugawa government built its first Western-style ship, a barkentine, at Uruga in 1855.[25] Several small two-masted schooners were built near Shimoda in the same and the following year, and the first Japanese-built steamer was completed at Nagasaki in 1857.[26] The construction of these ships seems to have been without benefit of direct help from foreigners. If so, these were the only wholly independent undertakings of the Tokugawa in this field; for the Tokugawa government, unlike the *han*, subsequently depended heavily upon foreign engineers and machinery to develop the shipbuilding and iron industries.

The policy of utilizing foreign technical aid, inaugurated with a naval training program under Dutch instructors in 1855,[27] was first applied to industry at the Nagasaki iron foundry. The equipment for the foundry was ordered from Holland, and upon its arrival in 1857 Dutch engineers and workmen were employed to supervise its installation. After 1861, when the plant was completed, Dutch employees were retained to provide technical guidance in its operation.[28]

The facilities at Nagasaki included a shipyard, and although a steamer was built there sometime shortly after 1857, the yard was used chiefly for repair work. The principal function of the foundry was the smelting of iron ore. Again, we have no data on output, but we know that the smelting facili-

---

24 *Mito han shiryō*, I, 97–98; *Zskzsr*, IV, 1111.

25 Takimoto Seiichi and Mukai Shikamatsu (eds.), *Nihon sangyō shiryō taikei* (*An Outline of Historical Materials on Japanese Industry*) (Tokyo, 1926–28), V, 642.

26 *Kzsj*, I, 339; II, 1450. *Nautical Magazine*, Nov. 1859, p. 569.

27 *Ibid.*, p. 568. Horie, "Bakumatsu no gunji kōgyō," p. 6.

28 *Ibid.*, p. 6. Ōyama, "Yōshiki seitetsu jigyō," pp. 2–4.

ties were large for the time; the foundry proper occupied an area of approximately 16,000 square yards.[29] An American physician gave the following description of the foundry in 1859:[30]

Dutch engineers are erecting a large machine shop for a steam hammer, and all the appliances needed for keeping the steam navy in repair. A steam engine is already at work moving lathes, at which apprentices, sons of men of rank [probably *samurai*], are turning, whilst others are molding, forging, or filing.

The repair facilities at Nagasaki soon proved inadequate. The number of Western-style ships was growing rapidly after 1858, as new ships were constructed and others were bought abroad, and it was found necessary to send the larger of these to Shanghai for repair.[31] Plans were made for additional repair facilities using equipment that had been purchased from Holland by Saga and given to the Tokugawa in 1859;[32] but after consultation in 1864 with the French minister, who emphasized the importance of large-scale construction facilities as a basis for naval expansion and offered to provide the necessary capital and engineering skill, the Tokugawa government decided upon a much more extensive program.[33] One new iron foundry was to be built at Yokohama and another together with a shipyard at Yokosuka.

In 1865 the Saga equipment was installed at Yokohama by a French engineer. The new foundry included workshops for making wrought iron, machine models, steam boilers, sails, and ship fittings, and for casting iron. The machinery used in the shops was powered by steam. It was intended that at least part of the equipment required by the larger Yokosuka foundry would be produced at Yokohama and that such farm implements and household articles as could be made from iron would be manufactured for sale.[34]

The Yokosuka foundry was planned on a much larger scale. In addition to the iron foundry, there were to be three ways for ship construction, two docks for repair work, and an arsenal; construction was to be spread over a four-year period at a cost of 600,000 Mexican dollars a year.[35] A French loan was arranged with the foundry serving as security, and a Tokugawa official was stationed in Paris to buy machinery and hire technicians. Actual construction was begun at the end of 1865 under Francis L. Verny, an engineer of the French navy, and two assistant engineers of French nationality; in addition, thirty-seven French mechanics were employed on the project. Con-

    [29] Ōyama, "Yōshiki seitetsu jigyō," p. 3. Honjō Eijirō, "Bakumatsu no kakushin teki shisō to seisaku" ("Reform Thought and Policy in the Late Tokugawa Period"), *Kzskk*, XII (Aug. 1939), 70.
    [30] *Nautical Magazine*, Nov. 1859, pp. 567–68.
    [31] Honjō Eijirō, "Reon Rosshu to bakumatsu no shosei kaikaku" ("Léon Roches and Reform Policy in the Late Tokugawa Period"), *Kzskk*, XIII (Jan. 1935), 15.
    [32] Etō, "Takashima tankō," p. 56
    [33] Ōyama, "Yōshiki seitetsu jigyō," pp, 7, 11.
    [34] *Ibid.*, pp. 7–9. Honjō, "Reon Rosshu," pp. 16–17.
    [35] *Ibid.* The Mexican dollar (*yōgin*) was the standard monetary unit of foreign trade; it weighed 27.075 grams and was 90 percent silver. *Kzsj*, II, 1600.

struction proceeded as scheduled despite the disturbed political conditions of these years, and the work was approximately half-finished at the time of the Restoration in 1867.[36]

An important feature of the new foundries, and one that provided a precedent for the Meiji government, was the program of language and technical training established in conjunction with them. The objective of the program was clearly stated in the "Draft Plan for the Yokosuka Shipyard":[37]

In order that the Japanese government may in future years replace the Frenchmen in charge of shipbuilding with Japanese, a school will be established at the shipyard to train persons of talent as engineers and technicians.

The training program at Yokosuka was conducted on two levels. *Samurai* were selected for training as "engineers" and were instructed in French by the chief interpreter and in technical subjects by the various department heads. Young workers at the foundry were selected by the French engineers for training as "technicians"; they were given instruction in their respective jobs in the morning and attended school in the afternoon for instruction in "drafting and other essential studies." The instruction at Yokohama was on a lower level: one hundred Japanese artisans were trained in Western techniques by French instructors. In addition, a language school was opened at Yokohama in April 1865, with fifty-seven students and five French teachers, to provide interpreters for the foundries, and six of the students were shortly afterward sent to France for study.[38]

IV

Many *han* were also active in shipbuilding; Satsuma, Mito, and Saga held no such monopoly in this field as in the processing of iron. By the Restoration, no less than fourteen *han* had either repair or building facilities, the chief of which were located at Ishikawajima, Kagoshima, Himeji, Tsu, Sabusawa, Hagi, Tomonotsu, Saga, Aomori, Shingū, and Nanao. Tosa completed a schooner in 1859 and is said to have built other Western-style ships after that date. Before abandoning shipbuilding in favor of purchasing foreign steamers, Chōshū built two schooners for her navy in 1859 and 1860. Sendai, Awa, Tsu, Akita, Matsuyama, Himeji, Shōnai, Tsugaru, Fukuyama, and Ōno all built at least one ship of either the schooner or barkentine type. At the end of the Tokugawa period all *han* together possessed a total of ninety-four Western-style ships, as compared to forty-four for the Tokugawa. The combined figure suggests how rapidly knowledge of Western ships was de-

---

[36] Ōtsuka Takematsu, "Fukkoku kōshi Reon Rosshu no seisaku kōdō" ("The Policy of the French Minister Léon Roches"), *Sz*, XLVI (July 1935), 12. Horie, "Bakumatsu no gunji kōgyō," p. 9. Honjō, "Reon Rosshu," p. 17.

[37] Quoted in Horie, "Bakumatsu no gunji kōgyō," p. 9.

[38] *Ibid.*, pp. 9–10. Ōyama, "Yōshiki seitetsu jigyō," p. 8. Ōtsuka, "Fukkoku kōshi," pp. 17–18.

veloping and represented a substantial beginning in developing a merchant marine.[39]

Despite the remarkable spread of activity in shipbuilding among the *han*, the leadership of Satsuma, Mito, and Saga was conspicuous. They were the only *han* to build steamers, and Satsuma and Mito built Western-style sailing vessels earlier and in greater number than other *han*. Shipbuilding in Satsuma and Mito, and Saga to a lesser degree, was distinguished from the efforts of the Tokugawa by an absence of direct foreign technical assistance and very nearly complete reliance upon the study of Western books.

Satsuma was the first *han* to build a Western-style ship. It had a particular interest in developing a navy by reason of its exposed position on the southern approaches to Japan and an important maritime trade with the Ryukyu Islands. This interest was evinced as early as 1848 when the Lord of Satsuma had a Dutch work on the steamship translated and again in 1852 when Satsuma built three model steamships based in part on this translation.[40]

With the change in Tokugawa regulations on shipbuilding in 1853, Satsuma drew up a program for the construction of twelve sailing vessels and three steamers. The first of these, a sailing vessel, was completed the following year. In 1855 three docks were built at Sakurajima, and three sailing vessels and a small steamer were completed there in the same year. The extraordinary energy with which shipbuilding was being pushed suggests the potentialities of the program had it been continued. However, shipbuilding ceased entirely after 1855, and during the remainder of the Tokugawa period Satsuma sought to develop her navy by the purchase of foreign ships.[41]

Mito was only a few years behind Satsuma in shipbuilding.[42] It had been among the first *han* to recognize the need for a navy and had been studying ship construction from Dutch works at least as early as the Satsuma translation of 1848. In 1854, the year following the removal of restrictions on shipbuilding, Mito began work on a shipyard at Ishikawajima that was to retain importance into the Meiji period.[43] The first Western-style ship built there, the *Rising Sun,* a sailing vessel, was completed in August 1856. Five additional ships were built at Ishikawajima before the Restoration. One of these was a steamer finished in 1866 after four years' work. It was equipped with a screw propeller rather than the usual paddle wheel, was ninety-seven feet long, displaced one hundred and thirty-eight tons, and was driven by a sixty-horsepower engine—an impressive engineering feat for the time, considering that the ship was built without the help of foreigners.[44]

[39] *Nihon sangyō shiryō taikei,* V, 664, 732; *Kzsj,* II, 1553–56. Etō, "Kōchi han no shinseisaku," p. 9.

[40] The translation entitled *Suijōsen setsuryaku* (*A Short Treatise on the Steamship*) was made by an Edo *rangakusha* and was supported in part by the Lord of Mito. Horie, "Bakumatsu no gunji kōgyō," p. 7. Tsuchiya, *Hōken shakai hōkai,* p. 502.

[41] *Ibid.,* pp. 503–4.

[42] Mito built a model of a Western-style ship from a Dutch book in the Tempō era (1830–44) and another in 1855. *Mito han shiryō,* I, 97, 115.

[43] *Ibid.,* p. 121.

[44] *Kzsj,* I, 41.

Unlike Satsuma and Mito, Saga made some use of foreign technical assistance in shipbuilding. Early study of the steamship was based on a model purchased through a Dutch merchant at Nagasaki in 1853, and three years later Saga ordered complete equipment for steamer construction from Holland. The expense of installation was too great and the equipment was given to the Tokugawa, to be used eventually at Yokohama. While delivery of the equipment was awaited, Saga employed a Dutch mechanic and under his supervision built a fifty-ton cutter. In 1861 a boiler was built for a steamer that had been purchased three years earlier. The boiler proved satisfactory and several others, including three ordered by the Tokugawa, were built in the next two years. Encouraged by this success, Saga undertook the construction of a small steamer which was completed in 1865, shortly before the Restoration terminated shipbuilding by the *han*.[45]

Not all modern enterprises founded during the Tokugawa period were strategic; Satsuma and Saga established enterprises that were primarily commercial. Like strategic enterprises, however, these were linked in origin to the crisis in Japan's foreign relations. The exceptional financial strain of developing the new strategic industries and expanding armaments made the discovery of new sources of revenue imperative. Many *han* had long engaged in commercial operations to supplement revenues from the land,[46] and it was natural for the most progressive of them to extend this technique to new fields.

Direct foreign aid was a conspicuous feature of the nonmilitary enterprises; indeed, it was a condition of their success. In 1868, the year of the Meiji Restoration, one hundred looms and spinning machinery totaling 2,640 spindles were purchased by Satsuma from the Platt Company of Manchester. The machinery was installed at Kagoshima by seven English technicians and production was begun the same year under their supervision.[47] The new spinning and weaving mill, which marks the beginning of the modern textile industry in Japan, was large-scale for the time: the machinery was powered by steam and two hundred workmen were employed at the mill, which had a capacity of nearly four hundred pounds of yarn a day.[48]

In the same year Saga contracted with an English concern for the joint exploitation of the coal deposits at Takashima. The technical and commercial

[45] Etō, "Takashima tankō," pp. 54–57.

[46] Most of the *han* governments monopolized the sale of certain important commodities within their territories; they also monopolized the sale of the chief products of their territories, shipping these to Edo and Osaka, where they were disposed of through merchants acting as agents. Satsuma provides an excellent example of this practice. Certain areas were designated in which all suitable fields had to be planted to sugar cane. In these areas the entire produce, after the payment of taxes in kind, was sold to the *han* at a fixed price, which was one-sixth of the Osaka market price in 1830 and one-fourth in 1853. The *han* then shipped the sugar to Osaka, where it was sold to the highest bidder among wholesale merchants. Takahashi Kamekichi, *Tokugawa hōken keizai no kenkyū* (*A Study of the Tokugawa Feudal Economy*) (Tokyo, 1932), pp. 57–59, 436–42.

[47] Tsuchiya Takao and Ōkazaki Saburō, *Nihon shihon shugi hattatsu shi gaisetsu* (*An Outline of the Development of Japanese Capitalism*) (Tokyo, 1937), p. 267. *Commercial Reports by Her Majesty's Consuls in Japan: 1875* (London, 1876), p. 101.

[48] Tsuchiya, *Hōken shakai hōkai*, pp. 507–8.

experience of the English company was undoubtedly advantageous, but it was the inability of Saga to finance the project independently that made the joint enterprise necessary. The English company was to provide the necessary capital for developing the mine, and repayment of 50 percent of the sum invested was to be a first charge against profits, which were thereafter to be shared equally. Under this arrangement a shaft was sunk by English engineers during the course of the year, the first coal was lifted in 1869, and a second shaft was sunk in 1871. The new enterprise was characterized by the use of a number of Western mining techniques: the coal was moved in the shafts by a steam-powered winch; steam pumps were used to raise water from the subsurface; and the shafts were lighted by "Western lamps" (yōtō). The scale of operations may be inferred from the fact that three hundred miners were involved in a wage dispute at Takashima in 1870 and that the interests of the English company were bought for $400,000 in 1874, when the Meiji government took over the mines.[49]

V

In the development of modern industry the Tokugawa and *han* governments anticipated several important features of the industrial policy of the Meiji government. Government ownership and management of industry were a salient feature of the early Meiji period and were partly the result of the new government's inheriting the enterprises developed by its predecessors; in extending the principle to new fields of industry, the Meiji government was following Tokugawa example. In the operation of these enterprises, the Meiji government made use of foreign engineers and technicians, a policy already laid down in the Tokugawa period; and it was likewise following precedent in supporting training programs both in Japan and abroad to provide qualified personnel who would take over technical and managerial positions from foreigners.

In an even more direct way the Meiji government owed much to the Tokugawa and *han* governments. It was not obliged to begin the process of industrialization from scratch. When the new government took power, it was already the prospective heir to several iron foundries and numerous scattered furnaces for smelting iron ore, a mechanized spinning mill, an important coal mine, scattered facilities for shipbuilding and repair, and a modest but substantial merchant marine. Not the least benefit of its inheritance was a group of persons who had acquired invaluable technical and managerial experience in starting these enterprises and upon whom it could draw for help. Thus by the end of the Tokugawa period the first and in some ways most difficult step in industrialization had already been taken, that of overcoming inertia and making a start.

[49] Etō, "Takashima tankō," pp. 6–8, 12, 14–17.

II. Political Change and Technological Innovation

INDUSTRIAL growth proceeds from a series of technological and organizational innovations in production that react differently on the stability of different kinds of societies. Where innovation and industrial growth are already under way, further innovation, while it may be temporarily disruptive, is essential to the long-term stability of society.

In such a society, past innovations have been adding steadily to per capita income, accustoming each major economic group to a continuously improving standard of life; consequently, as soon as the stream of innovation is shut off, each group to sustain its expectations must struggle for a larger share of a constant or diminishing output.[1] The static society—in the ideal case, one in which no significant change has taken place for a very long time—presents the reverse situation: continued stability requires that nothing of importance be changed. Since technological innovation cannot fail to create new functions and a new elite and to disrupt existing arrangements governing the distribution of power, wealth, and honor, all groups strongly favoring preservation of these arrangements must do their utmost to forestall or suppress large innovations. In the totally static society, then, a prerequisite to industrialization would seem to be the existence of a class antagonistic to and eventually capable of overthrowing existing arrangements.

I

Japan in the mid-nineteenth century was closer to the second model, the static society. The Tokugawa political system was based on a fine balance among nearly three hundred *han*. To maintain this balance, arrived at after a century of bloody civil war, every effort was made for over two hundred years to suppress growth and change. Japanese were forbidden to leave the country or to build seagoing ships, Christianity was suppressed, the country was cut off from all but a trickle of foreign trade, a secular orthodoxy was decreed for thought, society was frozen into a legally immutable class mold. But no regime can keep everything forever just as it is, and despite the most resolute efforts and refined methods to prevent it, Tokugawa society changed, obtrusively. Population, often a good measure of change, grew from about 18 million to about 26 million between 1600 and 1725; Edo, Osaka, and Kyoto in the same period all came to exceed 300,000 population; no less than a dozen ports, posting stations, and castle towns attained populations of be-

---

[1] "A steadily rising national income is the best assurance of harmonious social and economic adjustments. There can be no lasting harmony in a nation in which competing groups and interests seek to divide a constant or shrinking national output." Letter of transmittal; President Eisenhower's report to Congress. *New York Times*, Jan. 29, 1954.

tween 20,000 and 60,000 before 1700.[2] And behind these numerical changes lay structural changes, perhaps the most important of which belonged to agriculture. The radically altering ratio between urban and rural population induced three significant changes in agriculture. (1) There was a rapid growth of commercial farming and a concomitant concentration of landowner-ship and development of tenancy. (2) Accompanying these developments was a general and powerful growth of rural handicrafts, which made possible smaller holdings and higher rents. (3) Handicrafts were organized under the putting-out system by village moneylenders, landlords, and wealthy peasants, giving rise to a class of rural industrialists.

Feudal lords, sensing a threat to their agricultural base, did their best to suppress these changes, especially the development of rural handicraft industry. "In recent years," says a Tokugawa edict stating the reason for alarm, "agricultural servants (hōkōnin) have become scarce, and naturally wages have become high. Women weavers in particular get high money wages. Wages are high because labor is being used in secondary occupations and agriculture is neglected. . . . The utmost care will be taken that [peasants] devote themselves exclusively and unremittingly to agriculture and do not neglect their fields."[3] To assure that agriculture not be neglected, peasants were forbidden—depending on what it was that threatened agriculture locally—to grow mulberry trees, to sell raw cotton, to possess more than one spinning wheel, and so on.

Such prohibitions and restrictions were no more successful than other measures designed to make time stand still. Although such measures were not abandoned, daimyō slyly recognized their futility and learned to profit from developments they could not arrest. Favored guild merchants were given exclusive rights to buy the products of local handicraft industry, and the lord, who created and enforced these rights, shared in the merchants' monopoly profits under arrangements that varied from place to place.[4] There was furious peasant resistance to these monopolies and significantly it came from the upper stratum of the peasantry;[5] but we shall return later to the alienation of this dominant peasant class.

So while radical changes were taking place in Tokugawa society, there was a disposition on the part of the shogunate and han governments to resist them where this was possible and to exploit them where it was not. In either case innovations of the order industrialization required were unlikely if not

[2] Sekiyama Naotarō, Kinsei nihon jinkō no kenkyū (A Study of Japanese Population in the Tokugawa Period) (Tokyo, 1948), p. 54. Furushima Toshio, Kinsei ni okeru shōgyō-teki nōgyō no tenkai (The Development of Commercial Agriculture in the To-kugawa Period) (Tokyo, 1950), pp. 18–19.

[3] Quoted in Shinobu Seizaburō, Kindai nihon sangyō shi josetsu (An Introduction to the History of Modern Japanese Industry) (Tokyo, 1942), p. 3.

[4] The best general study of this subject is Horie Yasuzō, Waga kuni kinsei sembai seido (The Monopoly Sales System in the Tokugawa Period) (Tokyo, 1942).

[5] For example, Hirozawa Kiyoto, Kinsei minami Shinano nōson no kenkyū (A Study of Agricultural Villages in Southern Shinano During the Tokugawa Period) (Tokyo, 1951), pp. 119–29.

impossible. It is true the Tokugawa and *han* governments introduced elements of modern technology between 1850 and 1868—although tardily and under extreme duress; but so did the Chinese during the T'ung-chih period (1862–75). And like the Ch'ing the Tokugawa stopped short of institutional reform, for the same reasons: the new technology was designed to defend, not subvert, existing institutions and values; and because it was, the seed of innovation fell on sterile soil in both cases. No more than a Chinese government that insisted on harnessing Western technology to Confucian institutions could the Tokugawa and *han* promote industrialization effectively while maintaining the feudal structure. Maintenance of the warrior class continued to take the surplus of society, leaving little for investment; the feudal dispersion of political power made impossible central planning and effective mobilization of the nation's resources; the closed class system smothered creative energies and tended to freeze labor and talent in traditional occupations. To sweep away these obstacles to industrial development was unthinkable: they were essential parts of a system that conferred power and (perhaps more important) they were worthy ends in themselves. In their attempts to import Western military technology Tokugawa officials made implicitly the same distinction between means and ends as Chinese Confucianists made explicit in the *t'i-yung* formula, "Chinese learning for the base, Western learning for use." But whereas the Chinese got stuck with this distinction, the Japanese were liberated from it by a revolutionary class that came to power in 1868. For this class there was no Chinese analogue.

We need not tell here the story of how low-ranking *samurai* seized power and used it. It is enough to note: (1) that the new government was highly centralized and immeasurably more powerful than the one it replaced; and (2) that for it there was little standing in the way of technological modernization that was sacred, including privileges of the warrior class itself. These two features of the new regime—centralized power and ruthless utilitarianism—go far toward explaining Japan's rapid industrialization; but they themselves need explanation. (1) Since the revolutionary *samurai* were low-ranking and for the most part impoverished (this was one of the sources of their dissatisfaction), whence came the strength by which they seized and held political power? And (2) having seized power, why, instead of destroying the feudal system, did they not revamp it along lines better to their liking, as many of their members wished?

II

Let me outline a possible answer in the broadest terms and then turn to the evidence for it. The dissatisfied wing of the warrior class was strong enough to overthrow the Tokugawa regime because it was allied with wealthy landlords, merchants, and industrialists who dominated the rural economy and controlled village government. This class, at least in some parts of the country, had revolutionary inclinations for at least two reasons. First, further development of its commercial and industrial activity was seriously impeded by restrictive legislation enforced on behalf of guild monopolists. Second, as commercial values penetrated and loosened the village social structure and tenancy spread, there was sharpening class feeling within the village, and the dominant class sensed that the enfeebled feudal governments (to which they were opposed anyway) were no longer strong enough to protect them. This class had not the status, freedom of movement, or self-confidence to assume leadership of a revolutionary movement; but it could support warriors who did, and it gave them more than support. To some extent it gave them direction, turning what might otherwise have been a struggle to reorganize the feudal system into a movement to destroy it.

Since the support wealthy peasants gave seditious warriors was necessarily covert and local, evidence of it is hard to come by; and what exists is either very general—leaving us with a desire for concrete cases—or so scattered and fragmentary one hesitates to generalize. But when we bring it together, there begins to emerge something very like a picture of peasant-warrior collaboration.

Take first the most general evidence of peasant participation in the Restoration movement. This is statistical data on the class origins (warrior, peasant, merchant) of Restoration leaders compiled from two volumes of biographies of persons given court rank posthumously between 1867 and 1927.[6] Our data include only men who were active between 1800 and 1867, that is, men who won their honors in the immediate pre-Restoration period; and, we must add, our figures on them are approximate rather than exact. The biographies are terse and they do not always make it absolutely clear whether a man was honored for his part in the Restoration or for something else; nor do they always tell us to what class he belonged. Ambiguous cases of these kinds, amounting to perhaps 10 percent of the total, introduce a subjective element into the compilation of our figures.

Now, keeping this in mind, consider the figures: 1,005 warriors, 132 peasants, 63 merchants, 152 whose class affiliation is wholly obscure, and 119 others (mostly doctors and priests). These figures are astonishing; and they become more so as we consider them closely. First, even though peasants to a greater extent than other classes, particularly warriors, participated in the Restoration movement *below* the leadership level, there was according to our data one peasant for every ten warriors outstanding enough to be given court honors. These figures, which reflect top leadership only, magnify the role of warriors as a class at the expense of other classes, particularly the peasantry. Second, if we define "peasant" broadly, as a person who held land and lived in a village, then many men whose biographies describe them as "warriors" or "merchants" were indeed peasants.[7] Of 583 warriors whose biographies I have checked on this point, 68 were *gōshi*: warriors who lived on the land and more often than not were merely wealthy peasants (usually

---

[6] Tajiri Tasuke, *Zōi sho kenden* (*Biographies of Sages Given Posthumous Court Rank*) (2 vols.; Tokyo, 1927).

[7] Ono Takeo, *Gōshi seido kenkyū* (*A Study of the Gōshi System*) (Tokyo, 1934).

headmen) who had been given the right to wear a sword and bear a surname for a generation. Moreover, most of the 63 merchants were rural, or at least provincial, merchants, and many of them undoubtedly could as well have been classified as "peasants" under our definition. Third, the two largest cities of the country, Edo and Osaka, where merchant capital was purest, least touched by agrarian interests, together contributed but three of the sixty-three merchants. This strongly suggests, although it perhaps does not prove, that the great city merchants were either neutral or sided with the Tokugawa; and that such outside help as the warrior class received came from the countryside.

What sort of peasant abetted warrior conspirators, and how, when, and where? We may as well say at the outset that these are not questions that can yet be satisfactorily answered; but there is evidence that throws considerable light on them.

First, most of the peasants who took an active part in the Restoration, as their biographies attest, were *gōnō*—wealthy peasants. They were peasant in the Tokugawa hierarchy of classes—warrior, peasant, artisan, and merchant; and in the sense that they lived in villages, their power and prestige were village-based (many were headmen), and they held land. But they were set off from the generality of peasants by more than wealth and power; for more often than not they let land to tenants rather than working it themselves and, perhaps more important, they frequently were moneylenders, merchants, or industrialists who put out raw materials and tools to handicraft producers.

Between this class of peasants and low-ranking warriors the social distance was not so great as is sometimes thought. Many headmen wore swords and bore surnames and claimed descent (often truthfully) from warrior ancestors; there was intermarriage between wealthy peasants and *samurai*,[8] and the two groups were brought together regularly by official business. But most significant perhaps, peasants with means and a desire for social distinction frequently hired *samurai*—undoubtedly poor ones—as tutors for their children; and considering the times it is hard to believe that education was not often political. We know that it sometimes included military training. Consider this passage from *Contemporary Observations and Hearsay* (*Seiji kemmon roku*, 1816) :[9]

Now the most lamentable abuse [of the present day among the peasants] is that those who have become wealthy forget their status and live luxuriously like city aristocrats. Their homes are as different [from those of the common folk] as day and night or clouds and mud. They build them with the most handsome and wonderful gates, porches, beams, alcoves, ornamental shelves, and libraries. Some give money to the *Shōgun* and receive the right to swords and surnames in return. . . . Others lend money to *daimyō* and local officials . . . and exercise in-

[8] For a case in point, see Nishioka Toranosuke, *Shōen shi no kenkyū* (*A Study of the History of the Shōen*) (Tokyo, 1935), pp. 825–30.

[9] *Kinsei shakai keizai sōsho* (*Collected Tokugawa Works on Economy and Society*) (Tokyo, 1927), I, 48–49.

fluence in their locality and abuse the common peasants. *Still others despise the minor local officials and win favor with imperial princes, members of the imperial family who have taken Buddhist orders* [monzeki], *and with people versed in court affairs.* . . . Moreover, village officials and others of wealth entrust cultivation to servants; they themselves wear fine clothes and emulate the ceremonial style of warriors on all such occasions as weddings, celebrations, and masses for the dead. . . . *They keep masterless warriors around them and study military arts unsuitable to their status*; they take teachers . . . and study the Chinese and Japanese styles of writing and painting. [Italics added.]

There is no reason to believe that this account of the wealth, pretensions, and influence of *gōnō* is exaggerated. There is plenty of evidence of fabulously wealthy peasants many of whom made big money gifts to warriors: to cite but one case, a peasant in Fukushima loaned the enormous sum of 1,032 *ryō* (principal and interest) to the *daimyō* of the Soma *han*.[10] Nor was a taste for letters rare among the wealthier sort of peasants, some of whom turned to subversive schools of learning. Muto Sanji, who was born in the late Tokugawa period, tells us that his father, an exceptionally prosperous headman, read the *Nihon gaishi* and that "His sense of duty to the Emperor was strong . . . and he often told me stories from the *Nihon gaishi* to encourage this sense [in me]."[11] As to what is perhaps most interesting in the quotation from *Contemporary Observations and Hearsay,* the alleged contacts between wealthy peasants and the imperial court, we can say very little. We learn from biographies that some of the 132 peasants given court honors after the Restoration studied in Kyoto under famous Confucian scholars and were intimate with *samurai* and *rōnin* politically active there;[12] such associations *may* have put them in touch with the court.

There can be no doubt about peasants studying military arts. As early as 1805 the *Shōgun* issued an order stating: "We hear that in recent times in the country peasants have retained masterless *samurai* and study military arts from them, and that peasants of like mind have banded together for practice."[13] We may be reading too much into the text to interpret "like mind" as meaning similar political views, but a later document suggests this interpretation. An order of 1863 to the "Great Watcher" (Ōmetsuke), head of the secret police, declared that *rōnin* were soliciting funds from peasants on the pretext of preparing to drive out the barbarians. "*Rōnin*," the order continued, "have become arrogant and reckless, claiming to act on order of the Emperor; and we hear that here and there *they are even enlisting peasants as confederates*."[14] (Italics added.)

[10] Fujita Gorō, *Nihon kindai sangyō no seisei* (*The Rise of Modern Japanese Industry*) (Tokyo, 1948), p. 112.

[11] Quoted in Ichihara Ryōhei, "Nihon-kata burujua riberarisuto no shakai keizaiteki jiban" ("The Economic and Social Base of a Japanese-Type Bourgeois Liberal"), *Keizai gaku zasshi* (*Magazine of Economics*), XXVI (June 1952), No. 6, 77.

[12] Tajiri, *Zōi sho kenden*, pp. 318, 326, 346, 358, 363, 437.

[13] *Zskzsr* (Tokyo, 1922), II, 1058.

[14] *Ibid.*, p. 1110.

In 1863, the son of Fujita Tōko, the Mito scholar, made a trip through Kozuke and Shimosa provinces to organize support for the imperial cause among the peasants. The *Hazan shimatsu*, a book written in 1899, gives this account of Fujita's trip :[15]

Fujita lived in Edo and went back and forth to Ogawa and Itako [now in Ibaraki Prefecture]. He laid plans with Takeuchi Hyakutarō and Iwaya Keiichirō of Akiji village to gather confederates [*dōshi*]. This Takeuchi was a rustic *samurai* [*gōshi*] who owned much property and was [locally] quite famous; Iwaya was a scholar under whom several hundred students studied. Since both were powerful men in the district, Fujita became intimate with them and planned with them to enlist confederates from neighboring provinces to carry out his objectives.

Jōshū being the place where the Nitta family had rebelled [against the Kamakura *Bakufu*], even now there were men who wished to serve the Emperor. But since the people were timid, Fujita decided to go to Jōshū to enlist sympathizers. Fujita, Takeuchi, Usui, Kobayashi Yukiire, Hata Yahei, and some ten others put out for Jōshū. First, they went to Nitta county, and then from Ota passed through Kisaki to visit Kanai Gorō. When they had explained their purpose of acting for the sake of righteousness [*gikyo no koto*], Gorō agreed immediately [to help them] and with him as a guide they went to Kiryū and Omama to enlist others. They also went to Shimosa and talked to sympathizers around Ashikaga. Oka Korinosuke, Utsunomiya, Sakagi Haruo expressed agreement and promised to help with a force of a hundred or so when the time came to act.

General as the language of this account is, it leaves no doubt of Fujita's subversive purpose, and it is significant that his effort to find collaborators centered among other places around Kiryū and Ashikaga, both important centers of handicraft silk production.

Education was apparently widely used to indoctrinate local youth. Take, for example, the activities of Sugita Senjurō, father of Sugita Sadakichi of Meiji political fame. The elder Sugita, who lived in a village in Echigo, where his family is said to have held 82 *cho* of land in the early seventeenth century, was a fervent supporter of the imperial cause and his home was a regular stopping place for pro-Emperor *samurai*, among them men as famous as Yokoi Shōnan. In 1857 Sugita established a school at his own expense, we may believe for a political purpose since the Fukui *han* because of the school stripped him of his office of Ōshōya, a kind of super village headmanship, and put him under house arrest.[16] Sugita was by no means alone in this kind of effort. In an article tracing the growth of "bourgeois thought" among the peasantry, Professor Shōji has compiled data on the sponsors of grammar schools founded in the late Tokugawa period in Fukushima Prefecture; of 521 such schools, 51 percent were sponsored by peasants (including headmen).[17]

---

[15] Shidan kai (ed.), *Hazan shimatsu* (Tokyo, 1899), p. 6.
[16] Ono Takeo, *Nōson shakai shi kōza* (*Lectures on the Social History of the Agricultural Village*) (Tokyo, 1942), p. 365.
[17] Shōji Kichinosuke, "Henkaku-ki ni okeru nomin shisō no mondai" ("Thought Among the Peasantry in a Period of Change"), *Rgk*, Nov. 1952, No. 160, p. 27.

It is possible that these schools did not teach a revolutionary doctrine, but we are inclined to think they did since there is evidence of imperial sympathies among educated peasants. *Shōya tekagami* (*A Headman's Hand-Mirror*), written by a headman in Iyo Province in 1813, suggests the link between learning and subversive ideology. In it, the author praises the imperial line and denies by implication the legitimacy of Tokugawa and *han* governments :[18]

Even the humblest people [the ruler] should treat compassionately, as one uses one's own hands and feet. When the enmity of the people is aroused, [the ruler] receives heaven's punishment and declines. Yoritomo took the empire, but because he relied on force and became extravagant, his line lasted but forty-two years and four generations. Amaterasu put virtue above all and the imperial line ruled in peace through numberless generations.

We must not imagine that dissident peasant leaders confined themselves to giving warriors moral and financial support; they also helped raise military forces and sometimes, even before 1867, put them to use. Perhaps the most famous of these forces—certainly the most dramatic—was the *Tenchū-gumi* ("Heavenly Avenging Force").

The *Tenchū-gumi* was assembled by conspirators in 1863 in Yamato Province. As to the organizational work that lay behind this feat—the force was composed of 2,000 *nōhei* (peasant soldiers) from four provinces—we are entirely in the dark. But the intent of the leaders is clear enough. They planned to attack and destroy the headquarters of the Tokugawa district magistrate (*daikan*) at Gojō, and then march triumphantly to Nara where the group would greet the Emperor, who was scheduled to make a procession to that city from Kyoto. This would dramatically identify the rebel group with the throne and, it was hoped, set off uprisings on behalf of the imperial cause all over the country. The plan miscarried. After burning the district offices at Gojō and putting the magistrate to death, the leaders suddenly changed their plans. Instead of proceeding directly to Nara, they marched on near-by Takatori castle, demanding weapons and other supplies. Upon being refused, the group assaulted the castle and was repulsed; and before recovering from this setback, troops from neighboring *han* arrived to crush the rebels and seize their leaders.[19]

What part did peasants play in this episode? We have seen that the soldiers of the *Tenchū-gumi* were *nōhei*. Moreover, peasants were heavily represented among leaders of the uprising if we count *gōshi* (rustic warriors) as peasants. From materials on the uprising, the historian of the *Tenchū-gumi* classifies the 75 leading conspirators as follows: 24 *samurai*, 18 *gōshi*, 10 peasants (5 of them headmen), and the rest doctors and priests and men

---

[18] Ono Takeo (ed.), *Kinsei chihō keizai shiryō* (*Historical Materials on Provincial Economy During the Tokugawa Period*) (Tokyo, 1931), VII, 173.

[19] Hara Heizō, "Tenchū-gumi kyohei shimatsu kō" ("A Note on the Rising of the Tenchū-gumi"), *Tosa shidan* (*Tosa History*), March 1938, No. 62, pp. 1–31; June 1938, No. 63, pp. 14–36.

whose status is unknown.[20] There is not the least doubt, either, that the leaders hoped for mass support from the peasantry and appealed to them in revolutionary terms. A manifesto issued immediately after the attack on Gojō stated :[21]

The magistrate of this district, Suzuki Gennai, whose intentions were intolerable, has been put to death. Despite the imperial wish to drive out the barbarians, [Suzuki] used the territory and people entrusted to him only to live luxuriously, thus harming the people and obstructing the imperial wish. Since the people of this magistracy henceforth come directly under [the rule of] the imperial court, they will honor the gods and protect the national polity which respects the ruler. In celebration of this occasion of returning to the original [way], this year's land tax will be reduced by half. As to future taxation, we wish to make it light, but an order will be given after consulting the Emperor. The above is to be announced to all the people without exception. Receiving such benevolence, be loyal !

A second manifesto promised that : "Those who join the *Tenchū-gumi* will be permitted to wear swords and bear surnames."[22] This promise of escape from social disabilities must have appealed to peasants well enough off to worry about such things. Shibusawa Eiichi, who rose from peasant origins to wealth and power as a banker in the Meiji period, recalls how as a boy "I determined that I must somehow cease being a peasant and become a decent human being."[23]

Another force of *nōhei*, less famous than the *Tenchū-gumi*, was raised by Chōshū *samurai* in collaboration with village headmen in Kawachi Province, an important center of the cotton industry. In October 1863 this force, which also numbered about 2,000, occupied the town of Ikuno, where the local magistrate was located, and before being crushed by troops from neighboring *han*, issued a manifesto promising a 50 percent reduction in the land tax and called for overthrow of the shogunate.[24]

III

Dramatic revolts against the old order were by no means frequent and they probably contributed little to success of the Restoration. But what is significant is not that these consciously revolutionary outbursts were few and abortive, but that they occurred at all. They reveal in a flash the subterranean sympathies of peasant leaders (*gōnō*) and show that they were prepared to sweep the old order away; and they confirm accounts such as Fujita's of a peasant-warrior alliance that we might otherwise discount.

No one can say confidently how important to the Restoration this alliance was. That it existed we cannot doubt; and in view of the need of the warrior class for powerful outside support we believe it was crucial. Since there is

[20] *Ibid.*, No. 62, pp. 4–5.
[21] *Ibid.*, p. 23.
[22] *Ibid.*, p. 24.
[23] *Ibid.*, p. 11.
[24] Emi Hiroshi, "Ikuno kyohei" ("The Armed Rising at Ikuno"), *Nihon shi kenkyū* (*Studies in Japanese History*), No. 20, pp. 28–39.

little evidence that city merchants contributed significantly to the Restoration and good reasons for thinking they did not, from what other group or class could this support have come? Moreover, an alliance with a nascent capitalist class among the peasantry helps explain the revolutionary use of power against the feudal system after 1867. It might be argued that nationalism explains this: that the Meiji leaders saw national salvation in modernization and hence in the destruction of feudalism. Undoubtedly they did, but why did they equate the power and good of the nation with new institutions rather than old ones, since the latter had given them a preferred place in society and the former did not? Contemporary Chinese patriots saw salvation in strengthening the old order, as indeed did many nationalist *samurai* who had helped overthrow the Tokugawa. The most plausible explanation, we think, is that the views of *samurai* leaders of the Restoration were colored by the interests and aspirations of their peasant allies; but, again, this is hypothesis, not established fact.

III. Motivation

EXTRAORDINARY men become entrepreneurs when they have the means and the will to innovate—when, to use Schumpeter's phrase, they combine successfully the factors of production in new ways. In the early Meiji period the government provided the means to innovate through its power to tax and borrow; men in the government provided the will. How they came by the will is something of a puzzle because their position precluded the usual motivation. Ambitious, restless, and imaginative as they were, the Meiji entrepreneurs worked for the state and self-enrichment was not their aim. Clearly they sought to enhance the power and prestige of Japan and incidentally, though not secondarily, their own. But this tells us very little. Throughout much of the nineteenth century Chinese officials sought the same ends for China and themselves by suppressing innovation rather than promoting it. The question is: why did the Japanese leaders believe industrial development would bring them closer to these ends? The suggestion has been made and widely accepted that the Meiji leaders thought of national power and prestige chiefly in military terms.[1] It was the military potential of modern industry that attracted them, so the argument runs, and they developed industry as part of a plan of military expansion. There is undoubtedly truth in this statement, but it needs to be put in the context of the social and economic problems thrown up by the Restoration and by trade relations with the West.

I

By commercial treaties negotiated in 1858 and 1866, Japan was thrown open to foreign trade, almost without restriction. Her tariffs were placed under international control and set at levels that exposed her backward agrarian economy to the full impact of the dynamic industrial West,[2] matching in unequal competition the power and precision of the machine with the strength and skill of human hands. Trade on these terms started the same disastrous cycle in Japan that it had elsewhere in Asia—a cycle that led through ruined handicrafts and financial instability to foreign political en-

[1] For a recent expression of this view, see Eugene Staley, *The Future of Underdeveloped Countries* (New York, 1954), p. 217.

[2] The commercial treaty of July 1858 was rather favorable, providing for a 20 percent ad valorem duty on all imports except a few specified commodities. However, the tariff convention of June 1866 deprived the Japanese of most of the protection the previous tariff had afforded. Specific duties, averaging about 5 percent ad valorem, were provided for a long list of goods including the most important classes of textiles. Gold and silver were duty-free; all other commodities were subject to a general 5 percent ad valorem duty. *Treaties and Conventions Between the Empire of Japan and Other Powers . . . Since March, 1854* (Tokyo, 1884), pp. 321–48, 768–69.

croachment. Loss of specie was the first signal that the cycle was under way in Japan and its meaning was understood.

Until the Restoration Japan enjoyed a tenuously favorable balance of trade, but the reasons for it proved ephemeral. One was that Japanese consumers were unfamiliar with foreign products—a condition that disappeared rapidly, particularly after 1868.[3] The other was that, during the first decade of foreign trade, European sericulture was crippled by a silkworm disease and Japanese raw silk and silkworm eggs had an almost unlimited market abroad.[4] With the abrupt recovery of French and Italian sericulture in the late 'sixties, and the preference for foreign products that Japanese consumers began to show about the same time, Japan's balance of payments suddenly turned unfavorable. Except for two years, imports exceeded exports continuously from 1867 through 1880, as Table I shows.

TABLE I

VALUE OF EXPORTS AND IMPORTS, 1859–80

	Exports	Imports	Balance
1859...........	¥ 578,907	¥ 543,005	+¥ 35,902
1860..........	3,234,560	2,996,568	+ 237,992
1861..........	2,343,755	2,198,406	+ 145,349
1862..........	4,468,141	4,054,169	+ 413,972
1863..........	4,751,631	4,336,840	+ 384,791
1864..........	4,782,338	4,433,720	+ 348,618
1865..........	6,058,718	5,950,231	+ 135,487
1866..........	8,681,861	8,393,766	+ 288,095
1867..........	8,575,822	10,445,888	− 1,870,066
1868..........	15,553,000	10,693,000	+ 4,860,000
1869..........	12,908,000	20,783,000	− 7,874,000
1870..........	13,543,000	33,741,000	−19,198,000
1871..........	17,968,000	21,916,000	− 3,948,000
1872..........	17,026,000	26,174,000	− 9,148,000
1873..........	21,635,000	28,107,000	− 6,471,000
1874..........	19,317,000	23,461,000	− 4,144,000
1875..........	18,611,000	29,975,000	−11,364,000
1876..........	27,711,000	23,984,000	+ 3,746,000
1877..........	23,348,000	27,420,000	− 4,072,000
1878..........	29,988,000	32,874,000	− 6,866,000
1879..........	28,175,000	32,953,000	− 4,777,000
1880..........	28,395,000	36,626,000	− 8,231,000

Source: Horie Yasuzō, *Nihon shihon shugi no seiritsu* (*The Formation of Japanese Capitalism*), pp. 108, 194.

These figures show an excess of imports in visible trade of approximately 67 million yen between 1859 (really the first year of foreign trade) and 1880.

[3] See below, pp. 26–27.

[4] Yamamoto Itsuji, "Tomioka seishijo setsuritsu to shoki no jōtai" ("The Establishment and Early Condition of the Tomioka Silk Mill"), *Rgk*, VI (Nov. 1936), 3–4.

The average annual excess of imports between 1868 and 1880 was 5,746,000 yen, a figure equal to nearly 10 percent of the average annual ordinary revenue of the government in these years.[5] The actual loss of specie was considerably greater than these figures suggest, for shipping, insurance, and other services not reflected in them were almost entirely in the hands of foreigners.[6] In any case, the loss of specie was sufficiently great for the *Kōgyō iken*, a massive official study of the Japanese economy completed in 1884, to report—with perhaps a touch of hyperbole—that foreign trade had completely drained the country of gold and silver. "What we send abroad henceforth," it declared, "will necessarily be what at the present time remains underground."[7]

The steady loss of specie had a disturbing effect on the currency and brought serious financial problems in its wake. While specie reserves were falling, the government had been forced to issue paper currency to meet the extraordinary expenditures described below. By 1880 the government held only 5 million yen in specie against more than 135 million in outstanding notes; this compared with 15 million in specie against 65 million in notes in 1874.[8] Since in the intervening years there had been no significant increase in productivity, the value of notes fell rapidly. The price of gold in terms of notes almost doubled between 1873 and 1881, and the price of rice in Tokyo rose from an annual average of 5.70 yen per *koku* in 1877 to 9.40 yen in 1879 and to 12.20 yen in 1880.[9]

Currency depreciation embarrassed the government in ways described in more detail later on; it will be enough to mention three of them here. First, about 78 percent of the ordinary revenue of the government in the period 1868–80 came from the land tax; and since the land tax was a money payment that remained constant from year to year, any depreciation in the value of money meant a corresponding loss of revenue to the government. Second, since any depreciation in the value of money reduced the peasant's land tax relative to his income, it tended to increase his purchasing power and encourage imports, contributing to a further loss of specie and a further depreciation in the value of paper money.[10] Third, rising prices had the effect of reducing *samurai* income, an important part of which consisted of interest on government bonds and consequently was fixed in terms of money.[11] The effect of in-

[5] See below, p. 74.

[6] Tsuchiya Takao, "Meiji shoki no bōeki seisaku" ("Foreign Trade Policy in the Early Meiji Period"), *Sks*, VI (Feb. 1937), 1370. *Tokio Times* (March 31, 1877), p. 154.

[7] *Mzks*, XVIII, 964.

[8] Horie Yasuzō, *Nihon shihon shugi no seiritsu (The Formation of Japanese Capitalism)* (Tokyo, 1938), pp. 173–74.

[9] The paper yen exchanged at its face value with gold in 1873; by 1881 one yen in gold would bring 1.843 yen in paper. Takahashi Kamekichi, *Meiji taishō sangyō hattatsu shi (A History of Industrial Development in the Meiji and Taishō Periods)* (Tokyo, 1927), p. 132. *Mzks*, XIII, 158.

[10] For the official view of the inflation, see Matsukata's memorandum of September 1881. *Mzks*, I, 433.

[11] Not only was the real income from bonds reduced; their market value fell off sharply, from 83.49 yen in 1878 to 69.50 yen in 1881. *Ibid.*, XI, 174.

flation on the *samurai* was particularly dangerous since this class was already under severe economic pressure and in some parts of the country in open rebellion against the government.

For all of these reasons members of the government were alarmed by the inflationary spiral and, rightly or not, regarded the loss of specie as its primary cause—or at least the only significant one the government could do anything about. Iwakura Tomomi told the Dajōkan, the supreme organ of the government, that if Japan's foreign trade was not balanced, national disaster lay directly ahead. Iwakura did not specify how disaster would come, but he was certain that "the very existence of our nation is in peril."[12] Maeda Masana, whose views always carried great weight, was of the same opinion. "If we do not immediately . . . balance our foreign trade," he wrote to the Dajōkan, "we will fall into a condition wretched beyond description. Specie will become more scarce, currency will continue to depreciate, prices will rise, and the strength of our nation will seep away."[13]

Since Japan's tariffs were under international control and could not be raised, there was but one way of reducing the flow of imports into the country. That was by driving foreign manufactured products, which accounted for the bulk of Japan's imports, out of the domestic market through competition, and to do this was one of the major aims of industrial policy throughout the early Meiji period. In 1875 Matsukata expressed the hope of the government in the new enterprises it was founding to compete for control of the home market:[14]

If we henceforth make every effort to increase production and reduce imports, we may confidently expect such growth of industrial production that after a decade financial stability will be achieved as a matter of course. If we fail to do this, however, and continue to buy imported goods with specie, our government and people may give the appearance of making progress but the reality will be quite different.

II

The storm signal of falling specie reserves was not as serious as what it portended—the ruin of Japan's handicraft industry through foreign competition. The bulk of imports, as Table II shows, consisted of consumers' goods that competed more or less directly with domestic handicraft products, and the competition was most unequal. Machine-made cotton yarn, for example, was not only stronger and more uniform (and therefore more easily woven) than domestic handicraft yarn, it was also much cheaper (Table III). Similarly, sugar imported from China was superior to domestic sugar; kerosene was less expensive and more efficient than vegetable oils and candles for lighting; imported woolens were cheaper and warmer than domestic silks.

The encroachment of imports on the market for domestic handicraft

---

[12] Tada Takamon (ed.), *Iwakura kō jikki* (*A True Record of Prince Iwakura*) (Tokyo, 1905), III, 633.

[13] Quoted in Tsuchiya, "Meiji shoki bōeki," p. 1370.

[14] *Mzks*, I, 284.

TABLE II

Chief Items of Import: Percentage of Total Imports by Value, 1868–82

	1868–72	1873–77	1878–82
Sugar and sugar products	9.37	10.67	11.30
Cotton and other yarns	19.29	16.73	23.67
Cotton cloth	16.39	18.93	15.71
Woolen cloth	15.97	16.74	14.40
Metals	2.30	4.63	6.01

Source: Takahashi Kamekichi, *Meiji taishō sangyō hattatsu shi* (*A History of Industrial Development in the Meiji and Taishō Periods*), p. 86.

products is reflected in the changing consumption habits of the Japanese people. By the first decade of the Meiji period, Western dress, food, and even architecture were common in Tokyo. A British consular official reported that in 1872 "The consumption in Yedo (Tokyo) of foreign goods appears to be very considerable. Almost in every street a certain number of shops may be seen where nothing but foreign articles are offered for sale."[15] Even in

TABLE III

Comparative Prices of Domestic and Imported Cotton Yarn per Kin
(1 *kin* = 1.32 lbs.)

	Domestic Yarn	Imported Yarn
1874	¥42.70	¥29.66
1875	43.54	29.94
1876	40.79	27.42
1877	40.41	26.86
1878	45.00	25.46

Source: Tsuchiya Takao and Okazaki Saburō, *Nihon shihon shugi hattatsu shi gaisetsu* (*An Outline of the History of the Development of Japanese Capitalism*), p. 270.

so remote a place as Hakodate, in Hokkaidō, there was in 1878 "not a thing [a foreigner] could wish for but is to be had at one of the Japanese shops."[16] A Japanese author writing in 1879 lamented the corruption of Japanese manners and taste by foreign products and ways, as follows:[17]

In former times the Japanese people made rice their staple food and ate vegetables and fish as a supplement. . . . Now, however, everyone knows the nourishment meat gives and some people who carry luxury to an extreme eat Western foods and drink Western liquors and even believe that the body cannot be sufficiently nourished by rice. . . . It used to be the custom to construct buildings of wood and spread straw mats on the floor. Under the Tokugawa, luxury was strictly forbidden and commoners could not build houses higher than three stories.

[15] *Commercial Reports: 1871*, p. 2.
[16] *Commercial Reports: 1876*, p. 2.
[17] Quoted by Takahashi Kamekichi, *Saikin no nihon keizai shi* (*Recent Japanese Economic History*) (Tokyo, 1934), p. 115.

. . . But now the architecture of government offices, schools, and factories imitates the Western style. . . . Thus we are importing luxurious habits along with the material aspects of Western civilization; our ancient habits of simplicity are being swept away. At first we despised the foreigners as barbarians, but now we venerate them. We compete with one another to adopt European and American customs, and this tendency in popular taste cannot be arrested.

Men in the government were more concerned with what was happening to Japanese handicrafts than with the corruption of Japanese manners. Iwakura warned: "With the exception of sericulture and silk-reeling, traditional Japanese industries are falling into decay";[18] and the *Kōgyō iken*, the government study mentioned earlier, confirmed his view in detail. The peasants of Toyama Prefecture, it reported, had for decades past imported raw cotton from western Honshū and spent the winter months spinning and weaving, but since 1880 the output of this industry had fallen over 50 percent.[19] Similarly, there had once been a flourishing sugar industry in Sanuki Province, but it had been ruined by foreign competition; now "neither producer nor seller is compensated for his labor."[20] The iron industry of Shimane Prefecture had all but disappeared as a result of the importation of superior metals from abroad,[21] and the importation of kerosene had had a disastrous effect upon the wax and vegetable oil industries of Ōita, Fukuoka, Shimane, and Iwate prefectures. In Ōita, for example, the wax tree had been grown on wasteland and the peasants had become prosperous making wax and candles from the nut. But the price of wax had fallen so low since 1874 that "the wax trees . . . [were] being cut down."[22] And so the report continues on the depressed state of handicrafts, prefecture after prefecture.

Handicraft industry was also hurt badly in some cases by the export of its raw materials. In Kawamata, Fukushima Prefecture, for example, there had been before the beginning of foreign trade approximately five hundred families engaged in silk weaving and they had produced approximately 60,000 rolls of cloth a year. By 1875 production had fallen to almost nothing because producers could not compete with foreign buyers for raw silk.[23]

To explain fully the economic and political significance of the depressing effects of foreign trade on handicrafts we must speak of the relationship of handicraft industry to agriculture.[24] Except for luxury articles, such as fine silks, ceramics, and lacquer ware, the market for which was little affected by foreign competition, handicraft production at the beginning of the Meiji

18 *Iwakura jikki*, III, 552.
19 *Mzks*, XVIII, 848.
20 *Ibid.*, XX, 169.
21 *Ibid.*, p. 79.
22 *Ibid.*, p. 213.
23 Shōji Kichinosuke, *Kawamata chihō habutae kigyō hattatsu shi (The Development of Habutae Silk Weaving in the Kawamata District)* (Fukushima, 1953), p. 40.
24 The best general treatment of this subject in a Western language is Takahashi H. Kohachirō, "La place de la Révolution de Meiji dans l'histoire agraire du Japon," *Revue Historique* (Oct. 1953), pp. 243–47.

period was predominantly rural, and it was carried on as an adjunct to agriculture. If we may judge from late Tokugawa documents, it was a rare village in which peasant families made nothing for sale during the slack periods in agriculture. Almost all documents of the class collected by Professor Nomura and known as *meisai-chō*, documents in which the headman reported on conditions in his village to the lord, mentioned handicraft industry of some kind. "When there is no farming to do," the typical *meisai-chō* reads, "the peasants of this village make straw rope"—or footgear, straw hats, yarn, cloth, candles, dye, paper, charcoal, sugar, soy sauce, bean paste, hardware, wine, salt, lumber—depending on the location and opportunities of the village. Some of this production was undoubtedly for home consumption, but since rarely more than one or two items were listed for any one village, clearly there was specialization and production was primarily for the market.[25] The *Chōbō fūdoki* (1841–51) lists twenty-seven handicraft commodities purchased by the households of a single village in Chōshū,[26] and we see much the same list of commodities bought and sold at a periodic village market at Aizu in 1665.[27]

Much rural industry was organized on a fairly large scale, suggesting that production was passing into the capitalist stage. We find, for example, the Tokugawa and *han* governments prohibiting the employment of labor for wages in rural industry, a sure sign that somebody was doing so.[28] Indeed they were: we encounter families in the village employing between five and ten workers at one handicraft or another and one case of a labor force of about forty.[29] There is other evidence of size, too. As early as 1718 a wealthy peasant family in Echigo was sending off to buyers in Kyoto a single shipment of cotton yarn worth 264 *ryō*; and a diary for 1756 shows a village headman in Aizu dealing in cotton, indigo, raw silk, cocoons, and rice wine, and brewing up to 356 *koku* of wine in a single day![30]

But however large the scale of organization became, actual production remained scattered under the putting-out system through individual peasant households. Peasant earnings from this employment did more than supplement agricultural income, they eked it out and therefore were essential to agriculture.[31] Tenancy, which was already widespread at the end of the

[25] Nomura Kanetarō, *Mura meisai-chō no kenkyū* (*A Study of Village Meisai-chō*) (Tokyo, 1949), pp. 159, 172, 191, 256, 268, 291, 327, 458, 526, 532, 575, 624.

[26] Toya Toshiyuki, *Kinsei nōgyō keiei shiron* (*A Historical Study of Farm Management in the Tokugawa Period*) (Tokyo, 1949), p. 81.

[27] Fujita Gorō, *Hōken shakai no tenkai katei* (*The Process of Development of Feudal Society*) (Tokyo, 1952), p. 235.

[28] Shinobu, *Kindai nihon sangyō shi*, p. 3.

[29] Horie Eiichi, *Hōken shakai ni okeru shihon no sonzai keitai* (*Modes of Capital in Feudal Society*) (Tokyo, 1949), p. 109. Yagi Meio, "Nihon ni okeru senki teki shihon no seikaku ni tsuite" ("On the Character of Early Capital in Japan"), *Rgk* (July 1948), No. 134, p. 41. Shinobu, *op. cit.*, p. 204.

[30] Kitajima Masamoto, "Echigo sankan chitai ni okeru junsui hōken-sei no kōzō" ("The Structure of Pure Feudalism in the Mountainous District of Echigo"), *Sz*, LIX (June 1950), 37. Fujita, *Nihon kindai sangyō no seisei*, p. 241.

[31] Toya, *Kinsei nōgyō*, p. 59.

Tokugawa period, had developed along with handicraft industry and, as is generally agreed, was sustained by it; for until this source of income could be added to that from agriculture no tenant could pay a high enough rent to make it profitable for others to let land to him. And just as tenancy had been built into the agricultural system by handicraft production, so had small holdings. For generations, where handicrafts were oldest, estates had been divided into holdings that were not viable except in combination with household industry, and by the Meiji period there was no turning back to the larger holding.

There was another way handicrafts were crucial to small holdings. The acquisitive capitalist spirit had invaded the countryside along with industry and trade, and in many villages common land had been divided and the individual lots were bought and sold, tending to concentrate in fewer and fewer hands in the process. With the disappearance of common land which supplied fuel, fodder, and fertilizer, the peasant family lost in self-sufficiency and required cash income, which on small holdings came almost entirely from home industry, to buy the things it could no longer take for the asking— particularly fertilizer.[32] It is not difficult to understand, then, that the depression in handicraft industry was no mere inconvenience for a few specialists; it shook the whole structure of agriculture to its foundations and the Meiji government with it. It affected alike rich and poor, landlord and tenant; and by posing the choice on small holdings between food and fertilizer, it even threatened to encroach on agricultural productivity.

That the early years of the Meiji period, when foreign imports were reaching flood tide, were a time of troubles for the peasantry hardly needs saying. Nor were the baleful effects of agrarian depression confined to agriculture. But the government could not work miracles: it could not, as the peasantry demanded, save handicrafts doomed by the machine. The government heard the demand, however. In the first decade of Meiji there were over two hundred peasant uprisings, more by far than in any ten years of the Tokugawa period, and these uprisings tested the mettle of the government.[33] Never in modern times has Japan been so close to social revolution as it was in the early 'eighties. All that saved the government was the social gulf between *samurai* and poor peasant. Had the discontent of the two classes flowed in one channel toward a single objective, there would have been little to remember of the Meiji government but its good intentions.

If the government could not work the miracle of reviving old industries, it could at least build new ones. Matsukata warned the Dajōkan in 1874 that if it did not the people would "lose their industries and fall into poverty and starvation," and he added gloomily that Japan would become a producer of raw materials for the industrial West.[34] Whom Matsukata meant by "the people" he did not explain, but we can guess. At the end of the 'seventies, no

[32] See family budgets in *ibid.*, pp. 42–69.
[33] Ono Takeo, *Nōson shi (History of the Agricultural Village)* (Tokyo, 1941), pp. 185–91.
[34] *Mzks*, I, 360.

less than 70 percent of the population was still engaged in agriculture as a *primary* occupation and this was the part of the population that was most directly hit by the falling off of handicraft employment.[35] It is difficult to single out motives for founding particular enterprises, but there can be no doubt that the hope of bringing relief to the hard-pressed peasantry was often among them. The Mombetsu sugar refinery, for example, was founded not only to help check the importation of sugar from China but to provide local growers with a market for their crop. The Tomioka spinning mill, the government announced, was built to provide employment, to encourage private spinners to mechanize their operations by showing them how, and so "to profit the people." Here the meaning of "people" is clear beyond doubt, since the spinning of raw silk was almost entirely a rural industry. Still another example of concern for agrarian interests is the Aichi cotton-spinning mill. When, in 1878, it was proposed to found a modern cotton-spinning mill in western Japan, it was decided to locate the mill in Aichi Prefecture because the need was greater there than in other cotton-producing areas in the west.[36]

III

A third problem that Meiji industrial policy was designed in part to solve was adjusting the *samurai* to a new society that had no room for a hereditary military class. The problem was at bottom economic and it was not new. It dates roughly from the seventeenth century when the *samurai* began to feel the adverse effects of commercial development. Rising prices and new luxurious tastes combined with ineptitude in handling money rapidly pushed the *samurai* into debt and, by the end of the Tokugawa period, the situation of the entire class was desperate. What commercial development had left undone was completed by the Restoration, which *samurai* hoped would bring them relief. The new government not only swept away *samurai* political privileges and most of their social honors, but also added injury to insult by liquidating their claims against the government with little more than token compensation.

Under the old regime *samurai* had lived on rice stipends paid them by the lord in return for military service. When the Restoration government abolished the shogunate and the *han* governments of the *daimyō*, it assumed responsibility for paying *samurai* stipends—it could not have done otherwise and stayed in power—but it paid them at a reduced rate. Even so, between 1872 and 1876 payments to *samurai* took annually from 25 to 100 percent of the government's ordinary revenue, and payments could not be continued indefinitely.[37] To put a term to its obligation and to reduce pay-

---

[35] Our estimate is based on the ratio of agricultural families to all families in 1888; the ratio for the period 1870–80 would probably be nearer 80 percent. *Daishichi tōkei nenkan (Seventh Annual Statistical Yearbook)* (Tokyo, 1888), pp. 76–77.

[36] Kinugawa Taiichi, *Hompō menshi boseki shi (History of Cotton Spinning in Japan)* (Osaka, 1937), II, 93–94. Hamamura Shozaburō, "Ishin zengo no tōgyō" ("The Sugar Industry Before and After the Restoration"), *Kzskk*, XX (July 1938), 16; and below, p. 62.

[37] Compare Tables IV and XV, pp. 32 and 74.

ments in the meantime, the government in 1876 commuted *samurai* stipends into interest-bearing bonds that matured in twenty years.[38] The annual interest payment on these bonds was approximately 50 percent less than the money value of the rice stipends they replaced, as Table IV indicates.

TABLE IV

AGGREGATE SAMURAI INCOME FROM END OF TOKUGAWA PERIOD TO 1876

Estimated value of rice stipends at end of Tokugawa period....... ¥34,621,583
Value of rice stipends in 1871 at current market price of rice........ 22,657,948
Annual interest payment on pension bonds issued in 1876.......... 11,568,000

Source : Takahashi, *Meiji taishō sangyō hattatsu shi*, p. 102.

If *samurai* incomes before the Restoration were inadequate to maintain the style of life *samurai* were accustomed to, they were generally below the subsistence level after commutation. The government was well aware of this and did not expect *samurai* generally to live on interest from the new bonds. Rather, it was hoped the commutation of stipends into negotiable bonds would put enough capital in *samurai* hands at one time to permit profitable investment in some branch of trade or industry.[39] This would solve the *samurai* problem and at the same time contribute significantly to the development of the economy. But *samurai* proved no match for either merchants or peasants, and most *samurai* who tried to make their way in business or farming succeeded only in losing their capital. It was not just that the *samurai* were poorly equipped by experience and education to compete in these traditional fields of enterprise; the times were unpropitious for new ventures since the economy was highly unstable and (in its traditional sectors, at least) contracting. Long-term prospects were good, of course, but the success or failure of a new enterprise is not ordinarily decided by the long term. Moreover, the value of the bonds held by all but a few very high-ranking *samurai* was inconsiderable, and the market value of the bonds was being forced down continuously by a depreciating currency (in which interest on the bonds was paid), leaving most *samurai* who invested exceptionally vulnerable to short-term fluctuations.[40]

Instead of rescuing the *samurai*, the government's commutation scheme ruined them. There were notable exceptions, of course, but judging from government studies made in the early years of the decade after commutation, the exceptions were remarkably few. For example, in 1884 *samurai* in twelve prefectures held but 23 percent of the bonds issued them eight years earlier,[41] and there is reason to believe that most of the bonds no longer owned by

---

[38] Yoshikawa Hidezō, *Meiji ishin shakai keizai shi kenkyū* (*A Study of the Social and Economic History of the Restoration*) (Tokyo, 1943), p. 233.

[39] Tsuchiya and Okazaki, *op. cit.*, pp. 27–30.

[40] According to Iwakura's estimate, only 20 or 30 percent of *samurai* who made an attempt at business or agriculture succeeded. *Iwakura jikki*, III, 544.

[41] *Mzks*, XVIII, 814–70.

samurai had been sold to meet current living expenses or had been sunk in unsuccessful business ventures. At any rate only 101 out of 6,196 *samurai* families in the old Hiroshima *han* lived entirely on income from property, and 2,701 had no income from property at all. And when these same 6,196 families were classified by three income groups, described respectively as having "enough to live," "barely enough to live," and "not enough to live," slightly over two-thirds of the families were put in the last two groups.[42] What the officials who made this survey considered "barely enough" and "not enough" we are not told, but we may be sure the *samurai* concerned did not interpret these terms more liberally than did the government.

There was earnest discussion of the plight of the *samurai* in government circles from the Restoration until after 1880, and, so far as the written record shows, no one so much as hinted that the *samurai* simply be left to their fate. They were an elite too valuable to the nation to be allowed to suffer demoralization and economic eclipse if these could be avoided. As Iwakura, who among important leaders was perhaps the most strident champion of the *samurai*, put it: "Except for this noble kind of men, our people will not be able to compete with foreigners for another twenty or thirty years or more." And again: "Without the *samurai*, our nation cannot embark on the road to progress, but must decline like Korea and China. Whether our nation prospers or not depends above all on the fate of the *samurai*."[43]

Iwakura's direst prediction of what catastrophes neglect of the *samurai* class would bring did not strike other members of the government as fanciful; almost to a man they were *samurai*, and they believed as resolutely as Iwakura in the unique qualities of their class.[44] They were all aware, too, of the immediate political danger of *samurai* discontent; indeed, the danger was on them before they had more than a taste of political power. Between 1873 and 1877 there were four major uprisings among *samurai*, all aimed at overthrow of the government; and the government very nearly did not survive the last and largest of these, the Satsuma Rebellion. The fighting ended nevertheless in a victory for the government so decisive that *samurai* did not again venture to challenge it with arms. *Samurai* opposition to the government did not cease, however; it now took the no less dangerous form of a political movement shrilly demanding a constitution and representative government.

Since the *samurai* problem was essentially economic, it called for an economic solution, as every government document on the problem stressed. There were but two possible economic solutions, broadly speaking: either the government had to support the *samurai* as it had in the past on a kind of dole, or it had to expand the economy sufficiently to make room for them as producers. The first of these alternatives was not seriously considered since it

---

[42] Yoshikawa, *op. cit.*, pp. 244, 246.

[43] *Iwakura jikki*, III, 546.

[44] See the quotation from Ōkubo on this subject, in Tsuchiya Takao, "Ōkubo naikyō jidai kōgyō seisaku" ("Industrial Policy During Ōkubo's Term as Minister of Interior"), *Kzgrs*, IV (Aug. 1934), 1231.

would have saddled the government with a terrible financial burden and forced it to abandon the ambitious program of modernization to which it was fully committed; expansion of the economy, on the other hand, was not only compatible with this program but essential to it. Solution of the *samurai* problem, therefore, was constantly linked in official memoranda with industrial and agricultural development, particularly the former. "In trying to create employment for the *samurai*," Iwakura wrote, "we must give first importance to the development of industry." Fortunately this was a task for which it was thought the *samurai* were particularly suited. Indeed, "With their strength of spirit nurtured through generations, the *samurai* are equal to any task."[45] It must not be thought, however, that the *samurai* were merely to manage the new industry, they were to provide part of the working force too, and this was not idle talk; over half of the workers employed in the government's Tomioka silk mill in 1872 were of *samurai* rank.[46] "Let those *samurai* with some capital be given financial aid by the government, those with ability be placed in charge of the new enterprises, those with physical strength be employed as workers, and within a few years production in different parts of the country will be sufficiently increased that all the *samurai* now idle will be useful producers."[47] So wrote Iwakura in support of a program of government loans to *samurai,* but the stress on solving the *samurai* problem through industrial development suggests that this was one of the chief aims of government industrial policy as a whole.

IV

As revolutionary leaders are likely to be, the Meiji leaders were desperately harassed men. They had come to power by destroying old institutions and impairing old loyalties, and, until these were replaced, their grip on power was necessarily nervous and insecure. But if their destructive work deprived them of the support of part of the past, it also saved them from the illusion that trapped Chinese leaders: that the past could be preserved intact. Having burned bridges, they had to go forward—to find new solutions rather than refurbish old ones. In essence their problem was to make the transition from a traditional to a modern society: to find a new synthesis that would bring a new social and political stability. There is no evidence in their writings that the Meiji leaders had any clear, preconceived solution to this problem, but they were committed to finding a solution because they were committed to remaining in power; indeed, having used power violently in revolution against others, they could not safely relinquish it. And they discovered their solutions piecemeal, by answering the specific questions history asked of them. The old society, already fatally weakened by their revolt against it, was being steadily undermined by external forces, and the evidence and dangers

---

[45] *Iwakura jikki*, III, 548, 551–52.

[46] See below, p. 59.

[47] Quoted by Yoshikawa Hidezō, *Shizoku jusan no kenkyū (A Study of Government Aid to Samurai)* (Tokyo, 1942), p. 250.

of the process were clear. Imports exceeded exports, handicrafts were being ruined, the *samurai* class was dangerously discontent. It was in solving such immediately pressing problems as these that the government's industrial policy was hammered out. It is true, of course, that the Meiji leaders were quite aware that economic strength was an element of military power, but this awareness did not dominate their thinking on industrial policy. After the treaties of 1858 and 1866, the challenge of the West was not primarily military, but social and economic; and it was this challenge that industrial policy had to meet. No doubt it strengthened the resolve of leaders that, in meeting it, they were creating the basis of military power; but had military power been the immediate overriding goal, the Meiji government must have devoted its resources to creating war industries, when in fact it shifted the Tokugawa emphasis away from them. And because it did, industrial policy brought social and economic and political as well as military strength, rather than merely piling up armaments a failing society could neither support nor use. Some may feel that since military power was the ultimate aim or in any case one of the ultimate aims, it makes no real difference that it was not the immediate goal. But in fact it made all the difference between successfully reaching the goal and falling disastrously short of it.

IV. Private Versus Government Enterprise

THERE was no conviction among the Meiji leaders that industrial development should in principle be achieved through government enterprise. As we shall see, the government continuously sought to induce private capital into the new industrial fields, but until after our period efforts to do so were conspicuously unsuccessful. The principal reasons for lack of success were: (1) the weakness of private capital, (2) the initial technical and organizational difficulties machine production entailed, and (3) the conservatism of private owners of wealth.

It is well known that commercial capital developed powerfully during the Tokugawa period, and we will not repeat here the story of its growth. It will be enough to say that by the end of the period there were, in Edo and Osaka and even in outlying areas, immensely wealthy merchants whom one would expect to encounter as the industrialists of the Meiji period. Many of these merchant families, most notably Mitsui, did in fact take a leading role in the development of industry, but in the early years of the Meiji period, when industrial development had to go ahead rapidly if government was not to lose its authority, merchants almost to a man stuck resolutely to traditional fields of activity—commodity speculation, trade, and moneylending.

One reason for the reluctance of merchants to turn to industry was the scale of investment required. Great as merchant wealth seemed to contemporaries in the Tokugawa period, it was not equal to the immense long-term investment railways, shipbuilding, and factories called for. The *Kansai tetsudō kaisha* (Kansai Railway Company) illustrates this point. This was a company formed under government inspiration by a number of wealthy merchants in 1871; by it the government hoped to build the Osaka-Kyoto line with private capital. To attract investors the government contracted with the company to build and operate the railway and to guarantee its owners 7 percent per annum on their investment. Even under these terms, however, the company was unable to raise more than half the capital required for construction of twenty-seven miles of line. The company was dissolved in December 1873, and the railway was built with government capital.[1]

The figures on banking capital between 1875 and 1880 suggest how weakly developed private capital was at the time. As Table V shows, the aggregate banking capital of the country was 2,450,000 yen in 1875 and 43,040,000 yen in 1880. The difference between these figures represents a remarkable increase of banking capital in five years—nearly 1,700 percent; but the increase does not mean, as it seems to, that there was a large reserve of capital idle in 1875 that had found its way into banking by 1880. The increase was very largely the result of the issuance of pension bonds to *samurai* and *daimyō*

[1] *Mzks*, I, 235; II, 188.

TABLE V
BANKING CAPITAL IN JAPAN, 1875–80

Date	Number of Banks	Aggregate Capital (Figures in 10,000 Yen)
1875.....................	4	245
1876.....................	11	2,050
1877.....................	37	2,452
1878.....................	139	3,885
1879.....................	152	4,211
1880.....................	151	4,304

Source: Tsuchiya and Okazaki, *Nihon shihon shugi hattatsu shi gaisetsu*, p. 112.

in 1876; these bonds could be exchanged at the treasury for bank notes to be used in the establishment of national banks. This accounts for the bulk of the increase in banking capital between 1875 and 1880, as is shown by the fact that *samurai* and the nobility (*kazoku*), who were mostly ex-*daimyō*, together held 75 percent of the stock of national banks in 1880.[2] In short, the increase in banking capital represented capital created by the government after 1875 and not capital that had been in private hands before that date.

We do not suggest, of course, that banking capital was identical with capital available for investment, but the two must have been of the same order of magnitude. If so, the above figures are suggestive when put alongside those for government industrial investment. Calculating from 1868 only, investment in government enterprises amounted to 18,649,000 yen in 1875 and 34,553,000 yen in June 1880, and both these figures are very conservative estimates; actual investment undoubtedly ran substantially higher.[3] This suggests that private investors were in no position to make any considerable contribution to industrial development during the first decade of the Meiji period.

Maeda Masana said as much in his introduction to the *Kōgyō iken* in 1884. In his opinion, all of the many reasons for Japan's unsatisfactory industrial progress could be reduced to a shortage of capital: as he put it, development was slow because "capital does not match enterprise (*jigyō*)." There was scarcely an official document proposing the establishment of a new government enterprise that did not argue that private capital was too weak for the undertaking. In March 1876 the Department of Interior requested permission of the Dajōkan to establish a woolen mill, stating that: "Although it is the natural task of private interests to undertake an enterprise like this, the project must be carried out by the government. How can our people at present undertake such a large and exacting enterprise that will require a very

[2] Tsuchiya and Okazaki, *Shihon hattatsu*, p. 113.

[3] These estimates are mine; for a discussion of how they were arrived at see below, pp. 105–14.

large investment?"[4] The Departments of Army, Navy, and Industry used this same argument in proposing in 1880 that the government undertake directly to develop the iron industry. "If we wait upon private interests," it was argued, "we will not be able to anticipate a time when we will have a satisfactory large-scale iron industry in this country."[5]

But as Maeda repeatedly stated in the Kōgyō iken, private investment in industry was deterred by other factors as well as the scale of investment industry in general required. There were enterprises such as iron foundries and railways for which private capital was manifestly inadequate, but there were others of which this could not be said—cotton spinning, for instance. Still private capital was not entering these fields. For one thing, interest rates were extremely high; in the Tokyo money market they averaged around 10 percent in 1882 and probably still higher outside the capital.[6] This tended to channel capital into speculative fields where quick profits were possible, and away from industry, which required long-term investment and could not be expected to yield a high rate of profit owing to foreign competition and initial technical difficulties. When there was investment in industry, enterprises were generally started with insufficient operating capital—a major cause of failures and a source of what Maeda called capital "wastage." Moreover, the high value placed on capital permitted investors to demand dividends from the very beginning of a venture, and this drove many otherwise promising enterprises into bankruptcy.[7]

Another factor tending to check industrial investment was the slowness, uncertainty, and high cost of transport. According to the Kōgyō iken, the cost of coastal transport per mile in Japan was about 400 percent higher than between New York and Hamburg and about 1,000 percent higher than between New York and Yokohama;[8] and except where railways had been constructed, the cost of overland transport in Japan compared even less favorably with rates in Europe and the United States. A survey of internal Japanese transport by the British consular service in 1877 showed that it cost .07 yen, on an average, to move a kin of freight 24.40 miles where there was neither rail nor water transport,[9] or, as Sir Harry Parkes put it, ". . . it costs as much to convey a ton of goods fifty miles . . . on the backs of men and packhorses, as to send it from Japan to Europe."[10] In the same year, the Tokyo-Yokohama line carried sixty million kin of freight over eighteen miles of track for 69,000 yen, or an average of .001 yen per kin.[11] Since there

[4] Quoted in Tsuge Kō, "Ishin zengo yōmōgyō" ("The Woolen Industry Before and After the Restoration"), Kzskk, XIX (May 1938), 520.

[5] Mzks, XVII, 25.

[6] Ibid., XVIII, 67.

[7] Ibid., p. 65.

[8] Ibid., pp. 67–68.

[9] Figures based on charges of the Tsūun kaisha, by far the largest overland transport company in Japan at that time. Commercial Reports by Her Majesty's Consuls in Japan: 1877, p. 104.

[10] Commercial Reports: 1881, p. 89.

[11] Mzks, XVII, 186–87.

were almost no inland waterways in Japan, no considerable industrial development could be expected until a national system of railways was built. The absence of rail transport except in the vicinity of Tokyo and Osaka cut off Japanese factories (mostly in prospect) from domestic raw materials and markets, and put them at a disadvantage in competing with foreign producers—in short, discouraged the building of the factories in the first place.

The technological problems of machine industry were another formidable barrier to private investment. Maeda mentions these difficulties repeatedly in the *Kōgyō iken*. "The Japanese people," he wrote, "are generally unaccustomed to handling foreign machinery. They are so ignorant of the science of mechanics that they cannot easily open an ordinary Western lock. Even if they order machinery from abroad, they cannot operate it and, moreover, with the blacksmith serving as a machinist and using nothing better than hammer and file as tools, even the slightest repair cannot be made satisfactorily." And again: "Manufacturers, seeing at a glance the advantage of machine production . . . build factories of various kinds and employ our artisans who are inexperienced with machinery. This is one of the reasons new enterprises are unsuccessful."[12]

There could not have been many failures with machine production because there were remarkably few private ventures this early, as the case of mechanized cotton spinning illustrates. This was to become one of the favorite fields for private investment and by 1900 the entire cotton-spinning industry was privately owned. The reasons for this are clear: spinning machinery was relatively inexpensive and there was a large domestic market for cotton yarn. Nevertheless private investors shunned this as other industrial fields (with the exception of silk reeling) until government enterprise had shown the way. There was but a single privately owned spinning mill built in Japan before 1880, and the difficulties experienced with it suggest why. The founder of the mill, a Tokyo merchant, ordered machinery for it from the United States in 1864. The machinery arrived in Japan in 1867, but difficulties in assembling the machinery, learning how to operate it, and training a labor force delayed the beginning of production until 1872. Even after production began, there were continuing technical difficulties that together with competition from imported yarn kept profits low. In 1878, the best year before 1880, the mill showed only a 5-percent profit, or about half of the current interest rate on loans.[13] When one considers that the capital invested in this mill yielded nothing from 1867 to 1872, and that investment in machinery entailed far greater risks than other types of investment, it is no wonder others were less venturesome than this Tokyo merchant.

Before the commutation of pension bonds in 1876, almost all of the private wealth sufficiently liquid to have been channeled into industrial investment was in the hands of merchants. One of the reasons it did not flow into this investment field was the generally conservative outlook of its owners. This

12 *Ibid.*, XVIII, 70.
13 See below, pp. 60–61.

outlook is well reflected in the "house laws" of merchant families, which ordinarily consisted of a series of rules designed to promote the prosperity of the house. As one would expect, these laws extolled thrift, sobriety, honesty, kindness to customers, and so on, but surprisingly they also extolled conservative virtues generally. For example, the merchant was warned to be ever modest in dress and demeanor and to eschew anything that might be interpreted as socially presumptuous. Not only was he not told to be alert to new business opportunities; he was in effect warned against them. He must not depart from the business practices of the past handed down through generations, and there was the hint that to do so would be disrespectful to his ancestors. Frequently he was explicitly warned against venturing into new lines of business, and he was always warned, usually in the first article of the "house laws," to stay safely within the limits of the law. We would not expect breaking the law to be recommended, of course, but the prominence given this caveat suggests something more than respect for the law and ordinary caution. It reflects a fear of taking risks, of venturing anything uncertain, which seems to have been the cardinal principle of the merchant class.[14] With this outlook it is no wonder the merchant did not break new ground for industry.

Another factor that kept the merchant from investing in machine industry was ignorance. Machine industry placed business in a new context that required new kinds of knowledge—of technology and production, of foreign tastes and markets, of shipping and landing and warehouse charges outside Japan, of international financial practices. The merchant knew almost nothing of these things, and he could not readily learn them. There was little in the traditional lines of business to help him, and he could not learn from books until the government had issued specialized texts for his benefit. Knowledge of foreign languages as well as foreign travel, which was already assuming significant proportions by 1875, was confined almost exclusively to the *samurai* class. It was no wonder, then, that as late as 1884 Japan's foreign trade was still almost entirely in the hands of foreign traders; according to Maeda, they alone were competent to conduct it.[15] Yamaji Aizan, an influential publicist, pointed out the unfitness of the merchant class for industrial leadership. "The keeping of account books, the operation of the abacus, the calculation of short-term profits—these are the strong points of the merchant. But for the great work of surveying world conditions, hiring foreign employees, and applying Western methods of management, the *samurai* is better fitted than the merchant although he is inexperienced in business."[16]

It was clear from the first years of the Meiji period that the many obstacles to Japan's industrial development could not be surmounted without government action of some kind. As Ōkubo Toshimichi expressed it: "Our

---

[14] Miyamoto Mataji, *Kinsei shōnin ishiki no kenkyū* (*A Study of the Attitudes of Tokugawa Merchants*) (Tokyo, 1942), pp. 181, 184, 198, 215, 217, 220.

[15] *Mzks*, XVIII, 74.

[16] Kada Tetsuji, *Meiji shoki shakai keizai shisō shi* (*A History of Social and Economic Thought in Early Meiji*) (Tokyo, 1937), p. 447.

people are particularly lacking in daring : to encourage them to overcome this weakness and to study industry and overcome its difficulties is a responsibility the government must assume."[17] Two general courses of action were open to the government: (1) it could develop modern industry directly through government enterprises, or (2) it could encourage private investment in industry by extending to investors various forms of state aid including technical assistance, subsidies, and easy credit. Actually both courses were tried during the first decade of the Meiji period, but the second—state aid to private interests—proved almost entirely ineffective. The unsuccessful attempt to build railways with private capital was but one of many failures with this method. Matsukata wrote in 1881: "Since the Restoration . . . the government has annually extended subsidies to the amount of about seven or eight hundred thousand yen, but none of the enterprises [receiving subsidies] has been successful."[18] Maeda confirmed this statement in the *Kōgyō iken* and went on to urge that subsidies be discontinued, comparing them to pouring water in a bottomless vessel and to fertilizing land without the implements to work it. Maeda's point was that private investors did not yet have the necessary experience to make a success of their ventures. "People who envision new enterprises," he wrote, "have the right spirit and worthy objectives, but without experience and proper planning, these bring nothing but failure."[19]

[17] *Ōkubo Toshimichi bunsho* (*Documents Relating to Ōkubo Toshimichi*) (Tokyo, 1928), V, 565.

[18] Fukushima Masao, "Meiji shonen keizai seisaku to shihon chikuseki no mondai" ("Economic Policy in Early Meiji and the Problem of Capital Accumulation"), *Tōyō bunka* (*Oriental Culture*) (June 1952), No. 9, p. 15.

[19] *Mzks*, XVIII, 91–92.

V. Government Enterprises

THIS and the following chapter survey government enterprise in those industrial fields in which modern technology was introduced before 1880. No attempt has been made to give a history of particular enterprises; the available materials are in most cases much too fragmentary. Rather, attention is focused on three questions of general interest to this study. (1) What were the government's reasons for entering the particular fields it did? (2) What was the magnitude of the government effort in these fields, as measured by the size and number of the enterprises founded? (3) In which of these fields was private capital also active, and how did private enterprises in these fields compare in size and importance with the government's?

Of the fields in which it was active before 1880, the government was most successful in developing communications, partly, no doubt, because its greatest effort was in this field. The leaders of the new regime saw immediately that administrative centralization, general economic development, and military efficiency all depended upon the modernization of Japan's communications. Shortly after the Restoration a "member of the government" pointed out to his colleagues the advantages of a railway between Tokyo and northern Honshū. Such a railway, he wrote, would "make it profitable to reclaim waste and uncultivated tracts of moor and plain, and a still more important advantage . . . [would] be that, in case of a sudden emergency, it . . . [would] be possible quickly to put down disturbances." The writer concluded: "Railways are . . . of the first importance for the prosperity and military strength of the country; and it is desirable that they should be introduced into Japan without delay."[1]

As one would expect, there was opposition to the proposal to construct railways. The most determined and influential opposition came from Saigō Takamori, whose outlook was generally conservative although earlier he had taken a leading role in the Restoration movement. Saigō argued: "If in our envy of the greatness of foreign nations, we rush ahead without regard for the limitations of our own strength, we will end by exhausting ourselves without accomplishing anything. We must immediately dismiss the matter of constructing steam railways and concentrate on increasing our military power."[2] Saigō, who did not argue against railways in principle but claimed only that they were premature, was unable to carry with him the clique that was then in control of the government. This clique consisted of Iwakura,

---

[1] "Memorandum on the Advantages To Be Gained from the Construction of Railways," *Parliamentary Papers*, LXX (1870), 97.

[2] Ishii Mitsuru, *Nihon tetsudō sōsetsu shiwa (Historical Sketches of the Founding of Japanese Railways)* (Tokyo, 1947), p. 138.

Itō, Ōkubo,[3] Ōkuma, and Matsukata, all of whom were enthusiastic supporters of railway construction. Matsukata, for example, claimed that the relative differences in economic development among Western nations were primarily the result of differences in railway development.[4] Ōkuma, who as Minister of Finance was one of the two or three most powerful men in the new government, asserted that the small percentage of cultivated land in Japan was "without doubt principally to be attributed to the . . . primitive methods of transport[ing] . . . productions from one part of the country to another, where they are needed and where a market for their sale may be found."[5]

But railway construction was costly and technically difficult, and despite enthusiasm and energy the government completed no more than seventy-six miles of line before 1881. Tokyo and Yokohama were linked by rail in 1872; Kobe and Osaka were connected in 1874, and the line was extended to Kyoto in 1877. In the following year, work was begun on a rail-water extension from Kyoto that would cut across central Honshū to link the rich agricultural district around Tsuruga, on the Japan Sea, with Osaka, Sakai, and Kobe, on the opposite coast. The project called for the construction of a line from Kyoto to Ōtsu on the southern shore of Lake Biwa and the construction of a line from Tsuruga to Nagahama on the northern shore. The Kyoto-Ōtsu line, which was built entirely by Japanese engineers, was finished in 1880, and the Tsuruga-Nagahama line was completed in 1884.[6]

Such was the total of Japanese railway building during the period under study. All of it had been done by the government although numerous schemes had been sponsored by the government to enlist private capital in railway construction. So cautious were private investors that capital was raised in 1881 for the first private railway, between Tokyo and Aomori, only after the government promised to build the line for the owners with engineers from the Department of Industry, to make the land owned by the company tax-free, and to guarantee the company a net return of 8 percent per annum for ten years on the line between Tokyo and Sendai and for fifteen years on the line from Sendai to Aomori.[7]

Americans in Japan at the time enjoyed making fun of Japanese railways, particularly of the scanty mileage.[8] But Japan's railways as they stood in 1880 were already an important asset to the country. Twelve engines, 56 passenger cars, and 158 freight cars on the Tokyo-Yokohama line alone carried over 2,000,000 passengers in 1880. Twenty-six engines, 110 passenger cars, and 255 freight cars carried over 3,000,000 passengers over 58 miles of track between Kobe and Ōtsu in the same year. These were respectable

[3] Iwakura jikki, II, 1011. Itō Hirobumi den (Biography of Itō Hirobumi) (Tokyo, 1940), I, 493. Katsuda Magoya, Ōkubo Toshimichi den (Biography of Ōkubo Toshimichi) (Tokyo, 1929), III, 530.

[4] Mzks, I, 518.

[5] Tokio Times, May 11, 1878, pp. 255–56.

[6] Mzks, XVII, 161, 188, 190. Ōkuma Shigenobu (ed.), Fifty Years of New Japan (London, 1910), I, 437.

[7] Tsuchiya and Okazaki, Shihon shugi, pp. 129–30.

[8] Japan Gazette, May 18, 1879, p. 57.

records, even by American standards.[9] But Japan's railways were primarily important for the promise they held for the future. Experience with them had already made Japan almost wholly independent of foreign technical assistance in the construction, operation, and management of railways and promised the rapid extension of the existing mileage. There was no longer any doubt of the economic value of railways. The cost of overland transport between Tokyo and Yokohama had been reduced by approximately 98 percent,[10] and it must have been obvious to the government that it could remake the economy of the country by further construction.

The construction of telegraphs went forward during the first decade and a half of the Meiji period much more rapidly than railway building, no doubt because it cost less and was technically less difficult.[11] Whereas only seventy-six miles of railway had been completed by 1880 and the two elements of the existing track were separated by several hundred miles of mountainous country, almost all of the major cities of Japan had been linked by telegraph. Thousands of miles of branch telegraph lines and scores of minor stations were still to be added, but the trunk lines were nearly complete.

It is unnecessary to trace the development of the telegraph system in detail. The salient features of development are adequately described on the accompanying map, which shows telegraph construction between 1869 and 1880 by two periods (1869–76 and 1877–80) with an additional period covering the five years 1881–85. Development is shown below in Table VI by another criterion—the total number of messages sent and received annually between 1871 and 1885.

TABLE VI

NUMBER OF MESSAGES SENT AND RECEIVED BY JAPANESE TELEGRAPHS, 1871–85

1871.......	19,448	1879.......	1,935,320
1872.......	80,639	1880.......	2,223,216
1873.......	186,448	1881.......	2,784,187
1874.......	356,539	1882.......	2,836,221
1875.......	212,819	1883.......	2,599,711
1876.......	680,939	1884.......	2,695,176
1877.......	1,045,442	1885.......	1,356,206 (first six
1878.......	1,272,756		months)

Source: *Mzks*, XVII, 249–52.

All of the telegraph lines shown on the map were owned and operated by the government. There were a few privately owned branch lines (not shown

---

[9] *Mzks*, XVII, 186–87, 194–96.

[10] See above, p. 38.

[11] There was also an element of policy involved. Ease of construction gave telegraphs greater immediate importance than railways as an instrument of administrative centralization. As a result telegraph construction proceeded at an accelerated rate during the *samurai* uprisings of 1874–78, whereas no new railway construction was undertaken during these years. Ōkuma, *op. cit.*, I, 434.

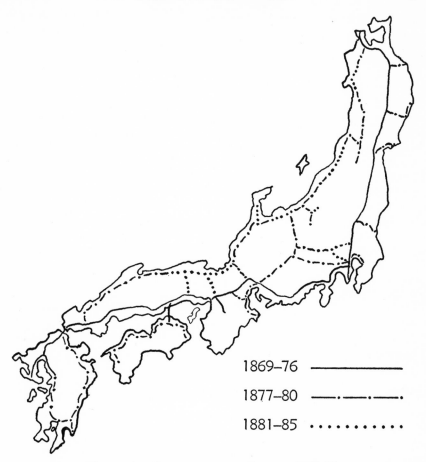

1869–76 ————————

1877–80 ——.——.——.

1881–85 ··········

TELEGRAPH CONSTRUCTION BY PERIODS, 1869–85

on the map) by 1885, but private ownership of trunk lines was forbidden by law. This prohibition was based on a concern for official secrecy, as the Dajō-kan admitted in rejecting the petition of a private company to build telegraphs in 1872:[12] "The nations of the West are thoroughly versed in our telegraphic codes. The establishment of a private telegraph company would therefore jeopardize official secrecy and interfere with the conduct of foreign relations."

Mining was a second field of industry that the Meiji government made a special effort to develop. An ancient belief in the fabulous mineral wealth of Japan persisted throughout the early Meiji period to spur on governmental and private mining activity.[13] But if expectations were not always solidly

[12] *Mzks*, XVII, 215.
[13] For examples of this belief, see Ōkuma's statement in the *Tokio Times*, May 11, 1878, pp. 255–56.

based, the government's objectives were sober enough. The government was concerned to locate and exploit deposits of precious metal and iron because mining was the most direct means of acquiring specie to balance foreign payments and iron was clearly a critical component of industrial and military power.[14]

The government had no such monopoly in mining as in communications. There were 4,563 private mines registered with the government in 1885; about half of these mined ores and the remainder were classified as "non-ore" mines—that is, salt, clay, oil, and so on. On the whole, however, private mines operated on very small scale. The 2,143 registered "ore mines" produced ore worth a total of 3,483,000 yen in 1885, or an average of 1,600 yen each.[15] The British *Commercial Reports* give some idea how these private mines were worked. In 1877 it was reported of Niigata Prefecture that although "copper exists in large quantities . . . copper veins are worked in a very imperfect manner by peasants of the localities where they are located."[16] Niigata also had considerable deposits of coal, but the British consul at Niigata thought only two coal mines in the entire district worthy of mention. One of these employed four miners and the larger, the Akatani mine, twenty. "Excellent" coal was produced at Akatani but methods were primitive.[17]

Coal was by far the most important branch of the private sector of the mining industry. Private mines in 1881 produced 99 percent of all coal mined in Japan, even though it must have been from scores of such tiny mines as Akatani that the coal came. If the British *Commercial Reports* are correct, there were but two private coal mines in the entire country equipped with modern mining machinery as late as 1877,[18] and the larger of the two, the Takashima mine, had been developed with foreign capital before the Restoration. Mechanization must have been even less advanced in private mines in the less developed branches of the mining industry.

Whereas there were thousands of small private mines in 1880, the government owned only nine, but these were equipped with modern machinery and were worked on a large scale.[19] Foreign engineers, geologists, and metallurgists were employed by the government; the Bureau of Mines had thirty-four foreigners on its technical staff in 1873, thirty-five in 1876, twenty-eight in 1877, and twenty-three in 1880. These men introduced Western mining methods—blasting, iron rails, steam power, mechanical drills—that private owners had neither the knowledge nor the capital to employ. It was a rare private owner who could afford the equipment an inventory showed at the government Kamaishi iron mine in 1882: fifteen miles of railway, two steam

---

[14] Kanda Takahira, "Tessan wo hiraku beki no gi" ("Why We Must Develop Mining") (May 1875), in Yoshino Sakuzō (ed.), *Meiji bunka zenshū* (*Collected Works on Meiji Culture*) (Tokyo, 1927–30), XVIII, 235. *Mzks*, XVII, 25.

[15] *Ibid.*, pp. 69, 87–88.

[16] *Commercial Reports: 1876*, p. 55.

[17] *Commercial Reports: 1878*, pp. 4, 71.

[18] *Commercial Reports: 1876*, p. 55.

[19] There is a short history of each of the nine government mines in *Mzks*, XVII.

engines, seventy cars for hauling ore, blast furnaces capable of producing seven tons of pig iron every twenty-four hours, and a ship (later sold for 170,000 yen) to transport iron and ore from the mine.[20]

With the benefit of foreign technicians and modern equipment, the six mines still being operated by the government in 1881 produced ore worth 1,444,000 yen in that year, nearly one-half the value of the total produce of the 2,143 private "ore mines" in 1885.[21] The size of these six mines is suggested by the personnel required to work them in 1881 : 404 officials, 3,360 workers above ground, and 3,775 miners, a total of 7,539 employees, or 1,256 per mine.[22] The over-all position that these six mines gave the government in the mining industry is shown in Table VII. By weight, government mines produced almost all the nation's gold ore in 1881, nearly one-half of its lead ore, and an important part of its iron ore. Private mines, on the other hand, produced almost all of the nation's copper and coal. It should be remembered, too, that these figures are for 1881 when the government was operating fewer mines than it had earlier.

TABLE VII
Mining Production, 1881

	Private Mines		Government Mines	
	Momme*	Percent	Momme*	Percent
Gold	33,129	10	281,211	90
Silver	2,498,353	9	25,182,656	91
	Kan*		Kan*	
Copper	1,201,246	94	77,889	6
Iron	3,112,005	77	944,933	23
Lead	41,220	59	29,720	41
Coal	201,211,707	99.006	83,838	0.094

* 1 *momme* = 3.75 grams ; 1 *kan* = 3.75 kilograms.
Source : *Daisan tōkei nenkan* (*Third Statistical Yearbook*) (Tokyo, 1884), pp. 129, 135–37.

The three most important shipyards of this period were all owned and operated by the government. Of these, the Nagasaki and Yokosuka yards had been built in the Tokugawa period and were merely expanded by the Meiji government ;[23] only one, the Hyōgo shipyard, was built entirely after the Restoration.[24] All three were something more than shipyards : to each was attached an extensive machine shop capable of making and repairing marine engines and boilers.[25] The "engineering works" at Hyōgo, for ex-

20 *Ibid.*, pp. 91–95, 134–37. Tsuchiya and Okazaki, *op. cit.*, p. 409.
21 *Daisan tōkei nenkan* (*Third Statistical Yearbook*) (Tokyo, 1884), p. 129.
22 *Ibid.*
23 See above, pp. 7–9.
24 *Mzks*, XVII, 316.
25 *Ibid.*, p. 312. *Daisan tōkei*, p. 156.

ample, employed an average of 232 workers a day in 1879–80 and was equipped with "several large machines, including a long-stroke planing machine, one large lathe . . . and a hydraulic riveting machine . . . and a new steam hammer."[26] The machine shops at Yokosuka, according to an American naval officer who visited them in 1877, were "well supplied with every modern appliance of machinery for successfully carrying out extensive engineering work."[27]

Of the shipyards proper, that at Yokosuka, which was given over entirely to naval construction, was the largest and best equipped. At least it was building larger ships than the others. Two of four naval vessels built there during the 'seventies were over 1,000 tons and a third was 897 tons.[28] Nagasaki and Hyōgo were used for commercial shipbuilding and repair. No description can convey so accurately the importance of these two yards as the construction records given in Table VIII.

It is impossible to say how many privately owned shipyards there were in Japan before 1880. We may be certain that there were some, although probably none rivaled any of the government yards in size and equipment. The official statistics on the Tokyo Metropolitan District listed three private shipyards in 1881. One employed 244 workers (about the same number as were employed at Hyōgo in the machine shops alone), another employed 153 workers, and the smallest 18 workers only; two of the yards, the largest and the smallest, were equipped with steam power.[29] It seems reasonable that yards of about the same size were to be found in or around Nagasaki and Osaka, the two other important centers of foreign influence, but we have no data on these areas.

Among the strongest motivations of industrial policy was the desire to balance Japan's foreign payments. This aim was particularly prominent in establishing manufacturing enterprises. In addition to textile mills, which we will treat separately in the next chapter, the government founded four enterprises of this class before 1880, and all were built primarily to reduce Japan's dependence on imports.

The Akabane *Seisakusho*, established in Tokyo in 1871, was one of the largest government enterprises of the time. Its purpose was to make machinery both for the government and private enterprise that would otherwise have to be bought abroad. The plant, which was powered by steam, consisted of an iron foundry, drawing office, and pattern, fitting, boiler, and blacksmith shops. By 1881 there was a labor force of 537 employed at Akabane, in addition to students from the government's Engineering College (Kōbu Daigakkō) who received practical training there. Among the things made at Akabane before 1883 were steam engines, boilers, girders for iron bridges, and machinery for sawmills, mines (rock crushers and drills), hemp and cotton spinning, silk reeling, and for manufacturing glass and sugar.[30]

26 *Commercial Reports: 1878*, p. 23; also for 1880, p. 18.
27 *Tokio Times*, Dec. 22, 1877, p. 348.
28 *Ibid.*, March 17, 1877, p. 121, and July 20, 1878, p. 40. Ōkuma, *op. cit.*, I, 226.
29 *Tōkyō fu tōkei sho* (*Tokyo Metropolitan Statistics*) (Tokyo, 1882), I, No. 85, 4.
30 *Mzks*, XVII, 306–8. *Tokio Times*, April 7, 1877, p. 166. *Daisan tōkei*, p. 145.

TABLE VIII
CONSTRUCTION AND REPAIR RECORDS OF NAGASAKI AND HYŌGO SHIPYARDS

	Vessel	*Construction* Year Completed	Burden (Tons)	Horsepower
Nagasaki:				
Steamships	1*	1872	70	Not known
	2	1875	92	60
	3	1879	212	60
	4	1880	297	65
	5	1880	67	20
	6	1881	53	18
	7	1881	200	75
	8	1883	970	175
	9	1883	15	15
	10	1883	224	80
Sailing vessels	1	1876	103	
	2	1882	336	
	3	1882	238	
Hyōgo:				
Steamships	1	1878	104	20
	2	1878	126	35
	3	1878	291	65
	4	1878	109	20
	5	1878	126	24
	6	1879	127	25
	7	1879	214	42
	8	1879	138	24
	9	1880	148	24
	10	1880	366	120
	11	1880	415	140
	12	1880	136	25
	13	1880	141	26
	14	1881	274	120
	15	1881	141	25
	16	1881	211	120
	17	1882	74	20
	18	1882	288	125
	19	1883	8	5
	20	1883	373	180
	21	1884	10	8
	22	1884	494	180
	23	1885	102	63
Sailing vessels	1	1878	235	
	2	1878	446	
	3	1879	1,227	

	Repair Total Number of Ships Repaired	Total Charges for Repairs
Nagasaki (1871–84)	297	¥314,428
Hyōgo (1875–85)	167	82,970

* Arabic numerals are used in place of the names of individual ships.
Source: *Mzks*, XVII, 315–16, 319–21.

Surprisingly, the other three manufacturing enterprises were to some extent by-products of foreign policy, which aimed at revision of the unfavorable treaties the Tokugawa regime had entered into in 1858 and 1866. One of the government's approaches to treaty revision might be called a strategy of flattery—to give proof of Japan's Westernization. Government officials and others prominent in public life, under prompting from the government, consciously set about aping foreign ways in everything from billiards to business suits. Part of the strategy was to construct all public buildings in Western style as symbols of the new era of enlightenment. An American lady visiting Tokyo in 1878 complained that "the government has vulgarized the new capital, making parts of it look more like the outskirts of Chicago or Melbourne than an Oriental city."[31] To avoid importing building materials for these new architectural monuments to the West, the government established the Fukugawa cement factory in 1875, the Shinagawa glass factory the following year, and the Fukugawa white brick factory in 1878. All were rather large enterprises for the time: each was equipped with steam power, and by 1881 there were 117 workmen employed at Shinagawa and a total of 83 at the two Fukugawa plants.[32]

As one would expect, manufacturing was the industrial field best developed by private enterprise before 1880. It was the one field of modern industry in which private enterprise outstripped government. Even so, the development of private enterprise was not impressive. The Tokyo Metropolitan District, which probably accounted for half of the modern industry in Japan, listed only 19 factories in its official statistics for 1881, exclusive of textiles and traditional branches of industry. With a few important exceptions these "factories" were small: only five were equipped with steam power, and nearly half employed fewer than 30 workers; the average capital investment (for 17 factories) was 30,927 yen, and the average gross income (for 12 factories) in 1881 was 47,763 yen.[33] Table IX summarizes the available data by factory and product.

The largest representative of Japan's military industry in this period was the naval shipyard at Yokosuka; in addition, the government operated two large works, one in Tokyo and one in Osaka, for the making of ordnance, rifles, and ammunition. These plants were supplemented by three small gunpowder factories, the Meguro and Itabashi factories in Tokyo and the Iwahana factory in Gumma Prefecture.[34] The only source collection on government enterprise, the *Meiji zaisei keizai shiryō shūsei*, contains no material on arsenals and ordnance works. Brief glimpses of these plants are afforded in descriptions by foreigners who visited them. As regards the gunpowder factories, we do not have even such accounts as these, and it is impossible to do more than affirm their existence.

---

[31] Isabella L. Bird, *Unbeaten Tracks in Japan* (New York, 1881), I, 35. *Mzks*, XVII, 308; *Tokio Times*, Feb. 10, 1877, p. 71; March 24, 1877, p. 135; May 5, 1877, p. 206.

[32] *Mzks*, XVII, 309. *Daisan tōkei*, p. 145.

[33] *Tokio tōkei*, No. 85, pp. 1–4. The *Statistics* notes that there were other "factories" (*kōba*) that were omitted because data on them were incomplete.

[34] Tsuchiya and Okazaki, *op. cit.*, p. 158.

TABLE IX

WESTERN-TYPE MANUFACTURING IN THE TOKYO METROPOLITAN
DISTRICT IN 1881

Product Manufactured	Kind of Power Used	Number of Workers	Capital Investment	Gross Income, 1881
Matches				
A	Steam	422	100,000	92,400
B	—	53	2,000	?
C	—	424	32,000	101,955
D	—	92	400	?
E	—	53	1,500	?
F	—	15	280	?
G	—	25	5,800	?
Leather*				
H	Steam	22	?	?
Paper*				
I	Steam	76	16,793	?
J	Steam	285	250,000	247,781
K	—	5	3,000	1,420
L	—	27	18,000	?
Lead pencils				
M	—	16	2,500	2,700
Scientific equipment				
N	—	18	6,000	21,120
Petroleum				
O	—	31	23,000	7,470
Pumps and other machinery				
P	—	13	?	8,500
Nails				
Q	—	15	3,000	3,590
Western-type candles				
R	—	8	1,000	7,000
Western-type umbrellas				
S	Steam	124	60,000	12,000

* The statistics give no indication whether the paper and leather factories listed were making a traditional or a Western product; but three of five factories in question used steam power and would therefore have to be considered Western-type enterprises in any case. Letters stand in place of names of individual enterprises; dashes indicate that the kind of power used is not listed in the source; question marks indicate that income is not listed.

Source: *Tōkyō fu tōkei sho* (*Tokyo Metropolitan Statistics*) (Tokyo, 1882), No. 85, pp. 1–4.

The American consul general, Van Buren, who visited the Osaka arsenal in 1880, found about 1,100 workmen employed there, principally in manufacturing cartridges for Snyder rifles.[35] The British consul at Hyōgo pro-

[35] *Commercial Relations of the United States*, Feb. 1881, No. 4, p. 221.

vided his government with a somewhat more detailed picture in 1874.[36] He reported:

Osaka possesses a large arsenal, where all kinds of guns are cast and gun carriages and appurtenances are manufactured. Saddles, bridles, harnesses, and all sorts of military accoutrements are made and beautifully finished after foreign models. The works in the establishment are carried on by Japanese artificers, unaided by foreign supervision whatever, and are very creditable to the Japanese government.

The editor of the *Tokio Times*, an American-owned weekly sympathetic to the Meiji government, was permitted to visit the Tokyo Arsenal in 1878. His account of what he saw on this visit is the only description of the enterprise we have.[37] He told his readers:

Passing from the West of [the administration building] . . . we soon reach the first of a series of substantial fire-proof edifices where various processes in the manufacture of arms and ammunition of war may be seen. A wilderness of lathes and lustrous metal turning into all shapes under the dextrous manipulation of the artizans bewilders the unprofessional visitor. . . . Next . . . we have perhaps the most interesting section connected with the arsenal, that in which the caps for various weapons are manufactured. Here are some ingenious and delicate machines, whose operation delights even the untutored eye. Near this shop . . . are several structures where the shells and cartridges are loaded. . . . Another large shop, where heavier machines are made, and whose busy wheels are moved by beautiful engines of French manufacture . . . made up the round.

The preceding survey brings out two important features of the early history of modern industry in Japan. First, a very modest beginning had been made toward industrialization by 1880, testifying to the difficulty of initiating the process; and, second, almost all of the modern industrial enterprises founded before 1880 belonged to the government. We are particularly concerned here with the second of these features.

The reasons for the dominance of government enterprise in the industrial field before 1880 are obvious. Not only did machine industry require large capital investment, but specialized machinery and technical skill had to be imported, production had to be organized on a large scale, and technical and managerial problems had to be worked out empirically. Private capital was much too weakly developed and too inexperienced to face problems of this magnitude. This is clearly suggested by the fact that private capital was least active in heavier branches of industry. Despite government encouragement of private enterprise, railways remained an absolute government monopoly until 1891, and private capital was almost as slow to develop shipbuilding and mining. There were a few private shipyards and hundreds of private mines before 1880, but with perhaps one or two exceptions in each

[36] *Commercial Reports: 1873*, pp. 21–22.
[37] *Tokio Times*, March 9, 1878, p. 130.

industry, all the larger modern enterprises were government-owned. Only in manufacturing did private capital show any considerable initiative. And even in this field private capital chose enterprises calling for no great outlay of capital and in which the productive process was not highly mechanized. Thus private capital invested in match and paper factories but shunned investment in the production of brick, cement, glass, and metals.

It seems clear that without government enterprise the beginnings of modern industry in Japan would have been delayed until after 1880, with perhaps disastrous results for the nation. It cannot be argued that government enterprise hampered development of the private sector of the economy. The government made persistent efforts to induce private investment in industry: government loans at low interest rates were offered to private investors, generous subsidies were offered to encourage private railway building, and government plants were used to work out initial technical difficulties in advance for private enterprise. The history of mechanization in the textile industry before 1880 will suggest why these efforts were abortive in other fields.

VI. Modernization in the Textile Industry

THE textile industry has special interest for us for two reasons. (1) If we understand the term "industrial revolution" in the narrow sense, as the mechanization of production and development of the factory system, then its first triumph in Japan was in the textile industry, as the data in Table X show. Of all factories listed in the industrial statistics for 1899, 56.8 percent were textile mills, which employed 62.8 percent of all factory workers. From

TABLE X

FACTORIES AND FACTORY WORKERS BY INDUSTRIES, 1899

Industry	With Power		Without Power		Total	
	Factories	Workers	Factories	Workers	Factories	Workers
Textiles	1,921	196,723	1,803	50,394	3,724	247,117
Machinery ...	208	18,412	157	4,205	365	22,617
Chemicals	190	12,966	650	25,625	840	38,591
Foods	207	8,584	605	15,239	812	23,823
All others	237	43,607	573	17,454	803	60,341

Source: Tsuchiya and Okazaki, *Nihon shihon shugi hattatsu shi gaisetsu*, p. 385.

the viewpoint of mechanization, the textile industry was also far ahead of others: textiles accounted for 69 percent of all factories equipped with steam or water power and 70 percent of all workers employed in such factories. (2) Whereas the government at the turn of the century owned and operated an important sector of other industries—notably communications, mining, chemicals, and metals—the textile industry was entirely in private hands.[1] Study of the textile industry, then, should reveal: (a) the highest degree of mechanization achieved in any industry before 1880, and (b) the maximum contribution of private capital in promoting industrial development before that date.

I

Cotton spinning and silk reeling were the two most important branches of the Japanese textile industry and those most rapidly mechanized and organized under the factory system. But there was a difference between the two in speed and mode of mechanization. Mechanization was much slower in cotton spinning and more dependent on government effort. The reasons for these differences are significant because they reveal the importance of government enterprise in the initial phase of Japanese industrialization generally. To understand these differences it will be necessary to note certain differences in the basic processes and economics of cotton spinning and silk reeling.

[1] Except for the government's Senjū woolen mill. *Kzsj*, I, 300, 923.

54

The mechanization of silk reeling was technically simple and comparatively inexpensive. Essentially, it required nothing more than applying power to the handicraft process, which was described in 1872 by the British consul at Hyōgo as follows:[2]

About 8½ lbs. of cocoons are taken and these are divided into thirty parts; one portion is put into boiling water and the thread reeled off first from five or six cocoons, increasing to seven or eight. . . . A small ring, made either of horsehair or human hair, is attached to the edge of the basin containing the cocoons and the hot water. The thread is run through this ring, and then passed in and out of the first and second fingers of the left hand, the right hand meanwhile turning the handle of the reel.

Mechanization of this process consisted merely in turning the reel by steam or water power, rather than by hand. The results of this simple innovation were striking: it permitted the reel to be turned at a faster and more constant speed, producing a silk filament of brighter luster, more uniform size, greater strength, and (because of these qualities) a higher market value. This left a critical and seemingly irreducible minimum of the total process to be done by hand. The cocoons had to be prepared, the filament started on the reel, and splices made when breaks occurred—all by ancient and expertly practiced hand techniques.[3]

The mechanization of cotton spinning was far more difficult and expensive. There was no intermediate stage between handicraft and machine spinning; machinery had either to be applied to the entire spinning process or not used at all. Spinning machinery was accordingly of an intricate, precision kind that was comparatively expensive and required a skill in operation not closely related to the technique of handicraft spinning.[4]

Economic as well as technical factors encouraged the more rapid mechanization of silk reeling. Silk reeling was based on a flourishing domestic sericulture that produced cocoons that were among the finest in the world. Moreover, silk reelers not only had an unchallenged monopoly of the domestic market, but a profitable and expanding foreign market as well. Domestic cotton, on the other hand, was coarse and short fibered and generally much inferior to foreign cotton. Indeed, cotton cultivation was a viable branch of agriculture only so long as it was protected by Tokugawa isolation. When foreign trade began in 1858, Japanese cotton production fell off sharply and finally almost disappeared. The Japanese cotton-spinning industry, then, as compared to silk reeling, was forced to develop under the competitive disadvantage of using an imported raw material. Moreover, from the beginning

[2] Commercial Reports: 1872, p. 58.

[3] C. F. Tweney and I. P. Shishov (eds.), Hutchinson's Technical and Scientific Encylopedia (New York, 1935), IV, 2161–62. Elliot C. Cowden, "Report on Silk and Silk Manufactures," Reports of the United States Commissioner to the Paris Universal Exposition, 1867 (Washington, 1868), VI, 28. Tsuchiya Takao, "Nihonmatsu seishi kōba no setsuritsu oyobi sōgyō jijō" ("The Establishment and Early Condition of the Nihonmatsu Silk Mill"), Kzgrs, Feb. 1939, p. 173.

[4] Tsuchiya and Okazaki, op. cit., p. 296.

it faced competition from English yarns, even in the domestic market. Competition was, of course, even more strenuous abroad where Japanese producers were handicapped by ignorance of foreign tastes and the intricacies of international trade; and it was not until nearly 1890 that Japanese producers ventured into foreign markets, even tentatively.

II

Paradoxically, the adoption of mechanical silk reeling was delayed for a time by the extravagant prosperity that foreign trade brought the Japanese silk industry during the decade after 1858. European sericulture had been suffering since 1840 the ravages of a contagious silkworm disease, and until French scientists checked the disease in 1869, Japanese raw silk and silkworm eggs enjoyed an almost unlimited foreign market. Under the stimulus of foreign demand, the Japanese silk industry experienced a period of extremely rapid growth: sericulture and silk reeling flourished in the traditional centers of production and spread to new areas where they had not been profitable before. So long as foreign demand continued high, Japanese producers reeled silk as they had always done and had no reason to change their methods.[5]

But the silk boom lasted only a decade. With the quick recovery of French and Italian sericulture after 1869, the demand for Japanese silkworm eggs fell off sharply and the world market for raw silk turned competitive. This marks a turning point in the development of the Japanese silk industry because hand-reeled silk could not compete with the machine-reeled product, as a pamphlet issued in 1870 by the Silk Supply Association of London attests:[6]

Until 1850 to 1860, when the silk worm disease assumed in Europe a serious aspect, the only fine and well-reeled silk produced in good quantity was furnished by France and Italy. . . . China, Japan, and India produced excellent cocoons, but the silk reeled therefrom [by hand] was generally coarse, clumsy, and uneven, and consequently of relatively low value. These remediable imperfections still prevail.

Furthermore, the competitive position of Japanese raw silk had been weakened by the artificial prosperity of the decade before 1869. Handicraft technique had deteriorated as it spread to new regions, and even in the older reeling centers quality had been sacrificed to exploit the brisk foreign demand. By 1870 the decline in quality was beginning to affect the market for Japanese silk. The *Japan Weekly Mail* remarked: "That some steps [to improve quality] are required is evidenced by the loud and increasing complaints made by buyers and manufacturers at home, both of whom lament over the gradual deterioration of Japanese silk. . . ."[7] To survive under competitive conditions, Japanese silk reelers had to mechanize their operations, and sericul-

[5] Yamamoto, "Tomioka seishijo," pp. 2–4.
[6] Quoted in *Japan Weekly Mail*, June 25, 1870, p. 290.
[7] *Ibid.*, Sept. 10, 1870, pp. 422–23.

turists who had raised silkworm eggs for sale abroad were forced to turn to reeling.

The first mechanical silk-reeling mill in Japan was established in 1870 by Matsudaira Tadayoshi, the former *daimyō* of the Maebashi *han*. As one of the centers of the Japanese silk industry, the Maebashi district suffered early and acutely from the revival of European sericulture. To meet criticism by foreign buyers of Maebashi silk, Matsudaira purchased reeling machinery in Italy and hired a Swiss technician to install it in an old *han* warehouse.[8]

Ōno, one of the greatest merchant families of the Tokugawa period, also made an important contribution to the early development of machine reeling in Japan. The family was probably the largest dealer in raw silk at the time and had profited handsomely from foreign sales during the decade after 1858. Finding the market for Japanese silk suddenly contracting, Ōno sought to improve the quality of his product by founding a number of mechanical reeling mills. The family established its first mill, equipped with Italian reeling machinery, in Tokyo at the end of 1870. Encouraged by the success of this mill, it established a second mill with one hundred basins at Kamisuwa, Nagano Prefecture, in 1873, and a third mill, twice that size, at Nihonmatsu, Fukushima Prefecture, in the same year. Still other mills were founded the following year at Miyata, Takagi, Okamoto, Matsumoto, and Izukawa, all in Nagano Prefecture.[9]

The spread of mechanical reeling after 1870 cannot be followed in detail. With few exceptions, the new mills were too small to leave traces in contemporary records; but it is certain that the adoption of machine reeling was rapid and widespread. During the years immediately after 1870, the British *Commercial Reports* on Japan gave increasing attention to silk reeled by "filatures on the European model."[10] By 1877 there was a "marked increase in the supply of filature silks" and it was noted that "the ready sale they have met with at high prices compared with other sorts proves how much they are appreciated in Europe."[11] So rapid was the spread of the new filatures that, according to an estimate of a British consul, about 20 percent of Japanese silk was being reeled by machine in 1878. The same consul described the kind of mills from which this silk came: "Numberless small filatures . . . [have been] set up through Shinshiu, Joshiu, and other places. . . . Most of these are located near a stream, and are worked by water power, some by a steam engine. The plant and machinery of the smaller ones are of the inexpensive kind."[12]

This description is confirmed in a general way by the first official factory statistics, gathered in 1881. These statistics, which include only silk mills

[8] Tsuchiya, "Nihonmatsu," p. 173. Tsuchiya and Okazaki, *op. cit.*, p. 299.

[9] *Ibid.*, p. 304. Yokoi Tokifuyu, *Nihon kōgyō shi* (*History of Japanese Industry*) (Tokyo, 1927), p. 152.

[10] The first notice of this type of filature was in a report from Hyōgo in February 1872. *Commercial Reports: 1871*, pp. 5–6.

[11] *Commercial Reports: 1877*, p. 57.

[12] *Commercial Reports: 1878*, p. 42.

with more than eighteen reels, list one hundred and nine reeling mills driven either by steam or water power, excluding government mills.[13] The British consul's estimate on the percentage of silk reeled by machine is borne out by the statistics on raw silk loaded for export at Yokohama between 1875 and 1880. Machine-reeled silk accounted for 7 percent of the total for 1875, 8.1 percent in 1876, 20.5 percent in 1879, and 30.4 percent in 1880.[14] These figures probably do not give an entirely accurate picture of the silk-reeling industry as a whole, for a somewhat higher proportion of machine-reeled than hand-reeled silk was exported. But it is clear that the reeling industry was undergoing a technical revolution in the decade after 1870; with the exception of communications, this was not true of any other branch of Japanese industry.

The Japanese government was as concerned as were private producers to maintain a profitable foreign market for Japanese raw silk, although it was concerned for somewhat different reasons. In 1869 the favorable balance of trade that Japan had enjoyed since 1858 disappeared quite suddenly and an excess of exports was not seen again until the middle 'eighties.[15] The continuing drain on specie reserves to meet foreign payments upset currency values and indirectly endangered the whole reform program of the government. To redress the imbalance in Japan's foreign trade became one of the most important objectives of government policy; and one of the quickest ways of effecting this was to modernize the reeling industry since raw silk was the most important single item of Japan's export trade. It was particularly important in the years immediately after the Restoration, as Table XI shows.

TABLE XI

RATIO OF FIVE MAJOR CLASSES OF EXPORTS TO TOTAL EXPORTS, 1868–82

(*Percentages Based on Value*)

	1868–72	1873–77	1878–82
Raw silk	56.89	45.97	43.20
Tea	24.48	25.86	21.99
Marine products	5.88	5.45	6.26
Cereals and grains	.00	3.87	5.52
Metals	3.48	2.57	2.57

Source: Takahashi, *Meiji taishō sangyō hattatsu shi*, p. 86.

Three modern reeling mills were established by the government before 1880. The first and largest was built in 1872 at Tomioka, a small village in the heart of the Gumma silk district. A public announcement in June 1872 explained the government's reasons for establishing the new mill. The an-

[13] Tsuchiya, "Nihonmatsu," pp. 175–76.
[14] Hattori Shisō and Shinobu Seizaburō, *Meiji senshoku keizai shi* (*Economic History of Dyeing and Weaving*) (Tokyo, 1937), p. 139.
[15] With the exception of the year 1876.

nouncement[16] made three points worth emphasizing because they hold as well for later government reeling mills: (1) the declining reputation of Japanese raw silk was resulting in the loss of foreign exchange, called in the document "a diminution of profit to the nation"; (2) the main purpose of the mill was not to profit the government; (3) rather it was to encourage the adoption of mechanical reeling by private producers. The announcement read as follows:

The product of Japan most sought in foreign trade is raw silk, the value of which amounts to an enormous sum [annually]. Foreign merchants value it highly and, because of their purchases, raw silk is of first importance in profiting the nation. . . . However it cannot be said that the traditional methods of production followed in the various districts excel. . . . Further, this year producers have taken advantage of the high reputation of Japanese raw silk to export inferior varieties. . . . Consequently, foreign merchants have come to dislike our silk, and its reputation has declined. This has not only caused great loss to domestic producers, but it has also entailed a diminution of profit to the nation.

When the reputation of our most important product was about to be destroyed, how were we to overcome this evil? The government, wishing to recover from this decline and to maintain the profits of the people, has built a large silk-reeling mill at Tomioka, in Kozuke Province, at great expense to the public treasury. Reelers and instructors have been summoned from France. Operations will commence from the summer months of this year and silk of the finest quality will be reeled. Consequently those persons who wish to reel silk will be permitted to enter the factory and observe the work of reeling and the operation of the machinery. Moreover, four hundred women will be employed and will be instructed solely in silk reeling. . . . The women employed by the government, after they have been given instruction in expert reeling, will be transferred to the various districts, where they may be used to teach silk reeling. The people must put doubt and suspicion aside and quickly seek this employment. Further, how is the government competing for profit with the people in starting this enterprise at great expense? By spinning high-quality silk, the government wishes only to give the people a profitable example.

The Tomioka mill was built by Hecht, Lilienthal and Company, a French concern, and the project was supervised by a certain Paul Brunat, who had managed reeling mills for the company in France and Spain. Brunat was assisted by a staff of eighteen European technicians, including four women reelers. The plant, which was equipped with the most modern French machinery, was completed in June 1872, and by January 1873 was employing over four hundred women operators who had been selected for their expertness as handicraft reelers. Over half of them, it is worth noting, were from *samurai* families. As they learned to operate the new reeling machinery under the supervision of Brunat's staff, they were transferred, according to the government's plan, to the new private mills that were being established at this time, as instructors. Under the rigorous factory discipline instituted by

[16] *Mzks*, III, 383–84.

Brunat, the Tomioka plant was operating so efficiently by 1875 that the contracts of the foreign employers were canceled, and the mill was placed under an entirely Japanese managerial and technical staff.[17]

A second reeling mill was established by the government in 1873, on the model of the Tomioka mill. The new mill, which was built in Tokyo, was somewhat smaller (48 reels) and was not used to train operators although its primary purpose was to stimulate the adoption of machine reeling by private producers. The mill was operated by the government until November 1874, after which it was leased by the year to a series of private concerns until June 1879 when the government resumed operation.[18]

The third government mill, the Shimmachi scrap-reeling mill (*kuzuito bōsekisho*), as its name indicates, was different from the two earlier mills. It did not reel silk from cocoons but was established to process and utilize the waste from mills that did. The technique of reeling silk scrap had only recently been developed in Europe[19] and it was completely new to Japan. Saseki Nagaatsu, an official of the Department of Industry, had seen the machinery that processed scrap filaments for spinning in Italy, and at his suggestion the government introduced the new technique to Japan. Machinery was purchased in Switzerland, and two Germans and a Swiss were employed to install and train Japanese workers to operate it. The new mill, built at Shimmachi in Gumma, was completed in October 1877 and was employing over two hundred workers early the following year.[20]

II

The Restoration found cotton spinning at about the same stage of technical development as silk reeling. Spinning was still a handicraft practiced mainly by peasant families as a secondary occupation to agriculture. But while silk reeling underwent rapid mechanization in the first decade of the Meiji period, cotton spinning remained almost untouched by mechanization. By 1880 there were scores of mechanized reeling mills but only three such spinning mills, and only one of these had been built with private capital. The other two were founded by the Satsuma *han*. Of these two, the mill at Iso in Kagoshima had been built by the Shimazu family before the Restoration.[21] The second Satsuma mill was established at Sakai in 1870 and, like the Iso mill, was equipped with spinning machinery imported from England. Confiscated by the government in 1872, the Sakai mill was used for much the same purpose as the Tomioka reeling mill. Although operators for private mills were not trained there, the Sakai factory was run as a model mill, to show prospective private investors what equipment was required for machine spinning and how production was organized. Then, in 1878, for reasons that are not clear, this effort was abandoned and the mill was sold to a wealthy

[17] Yamamoto, "Tomioka seishijo," pp. 2–38.
[18] *Mzks*, XVII, 303–4.
[19] Cowden, *op. cit.*, p. 34.
[20] *Ibid.*, p. 35. *Kzsj*, I, 875–76.
[21] See above, p. 11.

Kagoshima merchant who also purchased the Iso mill from the Shimazu family the same year.[22]

The history of the third mill suggests why it was the only mechanized spinning mill established by private capital before 1880. Its founder was Kajima Mampei, a Tokyo cotton merchant. Kajima and a group of associates ordered spinning machinery totaling 576 spindles from an American company in 1864. By the time the machinery arrived at Yokohama in 1867, Kajima's associates had withdrawn from the enterprise, and Kajima was financially unable to go ahead with it alone. Not until 1869, when Kajima enlisted the support of the Mitsui family, was this obstacle removed; and then the enterprise was stalled for another two years by technical difficulties. Two foreigners were hired to install the machinery, but both proved incompetent and had to be dismissed. A third foreigner, an American mechanic named Stevenson, finally succeeded in assembling the machinery after about ten months' work. Since the model mill at Sakai had not yet been opened, another delay ensued while Kajima experimented with operating the machinery, and the first cotton yarn was not finished until the end of 1872. After 1872 the efficiency of the mill improved rapidly. Annual production with the original spindles increased by over 200 percent between 1873 and 1878. But despite increasing efficiency, competition from imported yarn permitted only the smallest margin of profit. In 1878, the best year the new mill had before 1880, Kajima made a 5-percent profit on his original investment, which was about half the interest charge on loans in the Tokyo market at that time.[23]

A conference of cotton spinners held under government auspices during the 'eighties discussed the obstacles to private investment in the industry. The main points brought out at this conference are worth summarizing because they apply as well to the period before 1880. (1) Unless production were organized on a fairly large scale, which meant a large initial investment, operating expenses were very high and cut severely into profits. (2) Since the cost of coal was excessive, producers ordinarily had to rely on water for power, and they consequently suffered from periodic power failures and from the inconvenience of plant location. (3) Plants tended to be cut off from either markets or domestic raw materials by inefficient and costly transportation. (4) Since there was no carry-over of handicraft technique in machine spinning, Japanese operators were highly inefficient by Western standards. For example: "Our mules turn very slowly, two times while they turn five times in the West. If the rate is slightly increased, to three times, our operators cannot keep up. . . . This is not because their operators are strong and ours weak, but because our operators are unskilled and our foremen do not know how to supervise workmen."[24] In this conference we find raised, in

[22] Kinugawa, *op. cit.*, pp. 146–70. Tsuchiya, "Bōeki seisaku," p. 1380.

[23] Tsuchiya Takao, "Takinogawa Kajima bōsekijo no sōritsu keiei jijō" ("The Founding and Management of the Kajima Spinning Mill at Takinogawa"), *Kzgrs*, III (Oct. 1933), 70–99. *Mzks*, XI, 209–10.

[24] Sambei Takakō, *Nihon mengyō hattatsu shi* (*A History of the Development of the Japanese Cotton Industry*) (Tokyo, 1941), pp. 51–53.

one form or another, most of the main obstacles to development under private ownership in every industry except silk reeling: capital shortage, absence of external economies, and technological and organizational difficulties.

The three spinning mills—at Iso, Sakai, and Tokyo (the Kajima mill)— produced but a tiny fraction of all the cotton yarn consumed in Japan. They had an aggregate of only 6,224 spindles in 1877, not enough to reduce significantly the flow of foreign yarn into the country.[25] The American consul general estimated that 241 additional mills of the same average size as the three existing ones would be required to produce the amount of cotton yarn imported in 1878,[26] and his estimate was probably not far off. Cotton yarn was Japan's chief import and its importance was increasing: it rose from 19.29 percent of total imports (by value) in the period 1868–72 to 23.67 percent in the period 1878–82.[27] Increasing imports of cotton yarn alarmed the government: they were the chief reason for Japan's annual foreign trade deficit, which amounted to approximately 100 million yen in the decade after 1870. Moreover, cheap imported yarns were destroying an important handicraft industry, and as handicraft production declined, so did the market for domestic cotton, the production of which fell off from an estimated 37 million *kin* annually on the eve of the Restoration to 29 million *kin* in 1878.[28]

Since the government was forbidden by treaty to raise Japan's tariffs, the only answer to imported cotton yarns was to develop machine spinning.[29] To this end the government took three measures financed by part of a 10-million-yen domestic loan raised in 1878. (1) Spinning machinery totaling twenty thousand spindles was purchased in England in 1879 and sold on easy terms (fifteen years for payment, without interest) to private persons and companies. (2) An additional two thousand spindles were bought at the same time for the establishment of two additional government spinning mills. (3) Long-term loans were offered to anyone undertaking to import spinning machinery for production.[30]

Adoption of these three measures marked the beginning of a significant development of machine spinning in Japan. The two new government mills were completed respectively at Ohira, Aichi Prefecture, in 1881, and at Kamiseno, Hiroshima Prefecture, in 1882.[31] By the end of 1885 ten private mills had been established with machinery purchased by the government in 1879,

---

[25] Kinugawa, *op. cit.*, II, 2.

[26] *Commercial Relations of the United States*, Oct. 1881, No. 12, p. 216.

[27] Takahashi, *Meiji taishō sangyō*, p. 86.

[28] Kinugawa, *op. cit.*, III, 158–59.

[29] Ōkuma, *Fifty Years of New Japan*, I, 480.

[30] To encourage the development of machine spinning, the government loaned technicians as well as capital to private enterprise. Etō Tsuneharu, "Koyū no mengyō to yōshiki mengyō no ishoku" ("The Traditional Cotton Industry and the Importation of the Western Cotton Industry"), *Kzskk*, XIX (June 1937), 605. Katsuda, *Ōkubo*, III, 750–51.

[31] Kinugawa, *op. cit.*, II, 93–95. Yoshikawa Hidezō, "Hiroshima bōsekijo to Hiroshima menshi bōseki kaisha" ("The Hiroshima Spinning Mill and the Hiroshima Cotton Spinning Company"), *Kzskk*, XIX (April 1938), 1–20.

and three others with the aid of government loans. Five additional mills were founded between 1880 and 1885, either independently by private capital or with loans from prefectural governments. As compared to a total of three modern spinning mills with an aggregate of 6,224 spindles in 1877, there were twenty-three mills with a total spindleage of 89,520 in 1886.[32]

The Japanese spinning industry was still far from mechanized in the middle 'eighties, and the expulsion of imported cotton yarns from the domestic market was a remote goal. According to a study made in 1884 by the *Kyō-shinkai*, an association of Japanese manufacturers, 90.1 percent of all cotton yarn (by value) consumed in Japan in that year was imported; and of the cotton yarn produced domestically, only 23.3 percent (by weight) was machine-made, the remainder being produced by handicraft methods. Nevertheless, a start had been made that provided the basis for very rapid expansion in the years immediately after 1886. By 1890 Japan's total spindleage had increased to 277,895, an increase of more than 200 percent in four years. Earlier government aid was in large part responsible for this increase, as is shown by the fact that, in the same period, 1886–90, the total number of spinning mills increased by seven, or only 33 percent.[33]

Government mills had served as models for private enterprise, working out technical difficulties and problems of plant organization. But equally if not more important was the financial assistance government extended to private enterprise after 1878. It seems clear that without government help of both kinds, private capital would have been no more successful in developing machine cotton spinning in the decade after 1880 than it had been in the decade before; in short, in this field as in all others except silk reeling, the government was responsible for overcoming the initial difficulties of industrialization.

III

The manufacture of woolens, which in recent years has become an important branch of the Japanese textile industry, began with the government's Senjū woolen mill. Woolen cloth was known in Japan long before the Meiji period, having been imported in small quantities as early as the Ashikaga period. In the Bunka era (1804–18), sheep were imported from China and raised near Edo to provide wool for the Tokugawa family. But woolen cloth was a luxury even for the *Shōgun* and it could not have been manufactured on any considerable scale during the Tokugawa period: domestic wool production was insignificant and woolen yarn was not imported until 1874; raw wool not until nearly a decade later.[34] Woolen cloth and clothing, on the other hand, were imported on a significant scale from the beginning of the Meiji period. This was partly a result of the extravagant vogue for Western

---

[32] Kinugawa, *op. cit.*, II, 127–28, 131. Tsuchiya and Okazaki, *op. cit.*, pp. 272–78.
[33] *Ibid.*, pp. 277–78.
[34] *Nihon bōeki seiran* (*A Handbook of Japan's Foreign Trade*) (Tokyo, 1935), pp. 232–33.

dress in the first decade of the Meiji period. As the Japanese newspaper *Kinji hyōron* recalled in 1877 : "In the second and third years of Meiji the demand for foreign goods increased remarkably. Those who formerly looked upon them with contempt changed their minds and even adopted foreign clothes. Our men adopted the European style. They put on fine tall hats . . . and took to carrying sticks after discarding their swords. They dressed in coats of English fashion."[35] The importation of woolens was also encouraged by the adoption of woolen uniforms for civil officials and for the army, navy, and police. Woolen cloth accounted for 15.97 percent of total imports (by value) in the first five years of the Meiji period and 18.74 percent between 1872 and 1877.[36]

As we have seen, it was an established government policy to combat imports by developing domestic industry. To this end, the Interior Department founded a large sheep ranch in Shimosa Province in 1875 and petitioned the Dajōkan in March 1876 to establish a modern woolen mill as well. The petition[37] underlined a number of considerations relevant to the establishment of almost every government enterprise before 1880. (1) The primary objective of the proposed mill was to improve Japan's foreign exchange position by reducing imports; (2) the development of industry by foreign capital was rejected; (3) private Japanese capital was incapable of developing the woolen industry at this time; (4) it was necessary for the government to build and operate a modern woolen mill, to meet at least part of current demand for woolens and to stimulate further development of the woolen industry by private enterprise. The document is worth quoting rather fully.

As times change, the material requirements of the people change. Even taste in clothing has changed [in recent times]. It is for this reason that our imports of various kinds of woolen cloth have been sizable year after year. That this is so is clear from the schedule of imports and exports.

Foreigners have already remarked this, and in July of last year, 1875, an American insistently requested permission to establish a woolen factory. Owing to the fact that a detailed study had previously been made, we resolutely rejected the request, with the statement that we already intended to establish such an enterprise in Japan ourselves. Nevertheless, the project has been put off, and our statement may be belied, giving rise to a controversy.

In addition, the cost of woolen cloth for the army, navy, and police, as an official expenditure, is about 557,000 yen a year. Expenditures for woolen cloth by the generality of officials and civilians is incalculable. In the final analysis, we are sending enormous sums of money abroad senselessly, simply because the manufacture of woolen cloth has not been developed in Japan. To expend thus the vitality of the nation is intolerable.

Owing to the fact that sheep breeding has been started already and measures carried out to develop production with the objective of achieving self-sufficiency [in raw wool], we should establish a woolen factory also. Sheep grazing and

[35] Quoted in *Tokio Times*, Jan. 27, 1877, p. 46.
[36] Tsuge, "Ishin zengo no yōmōgyō," pp. 519–20.
[37] *Ibid.*

the manufacture of wool are mutually dependent and must be carried forward together. It is unnecessary to explain that they cannot be separated. . . .

Although it is the natural task of the people to undertake such an enterprise, there is no way to carry out this project except to make it a government affair. How could our people at present carry out a large and exacting enterprise that requires an enormous investment? It is necessary in the present state of affairs that such an enterprise be first established by the government. Thus the people may be given instruction and guidance. Although the woolen industry may be entrusted to private enterprise later, for the present we must take the short cut [of government ownership].

Even though wool may be purchased abroad temporarily, as factories develop, grazing will also develop and prosper. This goes without saying. In becoming self-sufficient in the various kinds of woolen cloth, we may also expect to arrest the enormous imports of woolens.

The petition received the endorsement of the Dajōkan and construction of the Senjū mill began in 1877. All the machinery came from Germany and was installed at Senjū by German technicians. When the new mill was completed in 1878, five of the Germans were retained to instruct the Japanese operators, who numbered one hundred and fifty in 1880. The British consul at Yokohama reported in May 1880 that samples of cloth from the Senjū mill were "certainly very good specimens," and he provided a description of the mill that gives some idea of its importance. He listed the equipment at Senjū as follows: one seventy-horsepower "non-engine," six carding machines, forty-two looms, six self-acting mules, eight fulling machines, five brushing machines, one sizing trough, two centrifugal pumps, two washing vats, two rising machines, eight shrinking machines, five teasers, and one steam presser.[38]

The Senjū woolen mill occupied a unique position among government enterprises. It was the only mill that introduced an entirely new branch of industry to Japan, and it was the only enterprise in the textile industry that retained its importance for many decades. The first machine silk-reeling mills were built by private enterprise, not by the government; and the importance of the few government cotton-spinning mills was quickly eclipsed by the development of spinning by private capital after 1880. The development of the Japanese woolen industry, on the other hand, was extremely slow; not until the end of the Meiji period did it reach a stage comparable to machine silk reeling in the early 'seventies or machine cotton spinning in the latter part of the 'eighties. Not only was the mill at Senjū the only woolen mill in Japan in 1880; it remained the most important element of the woolen industry until after the turn of the century.[39]

Textiles were the first branch of Japanese industry to be mechanized and organized under the factory system; and they were also the first branch of

[38] *Ibid.*, p. 521. *Commercial Reports: 1879*, p. 41.
[39] Tsuge, *op. cit.*, pp. 522–23.

modern industry to pass entirely into private hands. It is surprising, therefore, to find that what was true of other industries before 1880 held in large measure for one of the two major branches of the textile industry. Japan had only three modern cotton-spinning mills before 1880, and spinning, in so far as it had been able to survive the flood of machine-made yarn from abroad after 1858, was still a handicraft process. Machine spinning developed rapidly in the decade after 1880, but it did so only when the government undertook vigorous measures to promote it. Machine silk reeling developed earlier and under different auspices. Mechanization was already widespread before 1880 and it was accomplished almost entirely by private enterprise, but only as the result of peculiarly favorable circumstances not present in other branches of industry.

VII. The Financing of Government Enterprise

THERE was a long and essential commercial prologue to the industrial revolution in England and Western Europe. By 1750 trade had been expanding at something like a geometric ratio for at least three centuries. During this time such places as Canton, Goa, and Novgorod were linked to London and Antwerp, and the men who organized or invested in trade—bankers, stockholders, sea captains, merchants, and manufacturers—profited handsomely. The Dutch East India Company paid dividends ranging from 12½ to 50 percent during the first half of the seventeenth century, and its British counterpart paid as high as 334 percent on single voyages in the same period.[1] Thus, when technological progress, to some extent forced by the demand of commerce for more goods, made possible the organization of industrial production on a larger scale, the accumulated profits from trade were at hand to finance the undertaking. In England many merchants had already turned to manufacturing, and they had the experience, organization, and capital— at least in the form of credit—to become industrialists; it remained only for the steam engine to make them such.

Japan, however, when she entered upon industrialization in the middle of the last century, had been cut off almost entirely from the profits of overseas trade for over two hundred years. During this time internal commerce had developed promisingly, but the home market, sharply limited by an impoverished peasantry, provided poor fare for battening capitalists. True, wealth did tend in this period of peace and security to concentrate in the hands of speculators, moneylenders, and rice brokers, and the wealth of the merchant became the envy of the noble class. But Japanese merchants were not prepared to play the role of industrialists, as had the English merchants a century and a half before. Except perhaps for the greatest merchants, their resources were puny by comparison to those of their English counterparts. Moreover, in the time between the beginnings of industrialization in England and Japan, technology had taken great strides forward and the capital required for financing industry had assumed an entirely new magnitude. But it was not only capital shortage that prevented the Japanese merchant from investing in industry. The great merchant families of Edo and Osaka had become wealthy by manipulating the terms of trade through government regulation. Profits, in their experience, depended on political influence and the dominance of guild organization, upon restricting rather than expanding production; and because they had left the organization of handicraft industry to petty rural merchants and landowners, the Restoration found them wedded to traditional lines of business and without industrial experience. Indeed, so

[1] Louis M. Hacker, *The Triumph of American Capitalism* (New York, 1940), p. 59.

poorly prepared were they for the new era that two of the three greatest merchant families—Ōno and Shimada—went bankrupt within the first decade of the Meiji period.

As we have seen, it was because private capital was poorly prepared that government played so prominent a role in the initial stages of Japanese industrialization. Only through the government's power to tax and borrow could the necessary capital be raised for such large undertakings as the construction of railways and shipyards and factories. But the government's ability to create capital was severely limited by the relatively low productivity of the economy and the political dangers of cutting too deeply into consumption. Moreover, there were competing claims upon the government's resources; industrialization was but one aspect of a broad program of modernization designed to equip Japan for survival in the era that began with Perry's arrival. In these circumstances, how much did the Meiji government invest in industry between 1868 and 1881? From what sources of wealth was the necessary capital mobilized? And how great a burden did capital formation place upon the Japanese economy?

I

There are difficulties in the way of either a simple or exact answer to the first question. The problem of defining "capital investment" is sufficiently complex, and the incompleteness of our materials and the vagaries of government accounting add to the difficulties. The manner in which these problems have been handled must be made clear so that the meaning of the resulting estimate of government investment may be understood.

The Finance Department classified in its accounts certain expenditures on government enterprises as *kōgyōhi,* a term that might be translated as "capital investment." Since this category of expenditures, like others in the accounts, was not itemized in much detail, the sums shown under it usually must be either accepted or rejected in total; hence *kōgyōhi* becomes the core of our definition of capital investment. *Kōgyōhi* was officially defined as all expenditures on government enterprises made prior to the beginning of operations (except for expenditures on raw materials, which were charged to operating expenses [*eigyōhi*]) and expenditures after that time for the purchase of additional equipment or construction of additional plant.[2]

Now it is not possible to obtain a realistic estimate of total capital investment in a given period by totaling the sums listed under *kōgyōhi.* There are items appearing elsewhere in the accounts that may be considered as part of capital investment. For example, the interest payment on a loan the principal of which was invested entirely in government enterprise falls in this class. But since the number and variety of such items are considerable, it is not easy to formulate a rule of thumb for deciding which to include and which to leave out. Rather than attempt to do so, we have eliminated the smaller sums regardless of the items to which they refer, a procedure that will not

2 *Meiji zaisei shi,* I, 926–27.

influence our results substantially, and have decided individually on the inclusion or exclusion of the few items carrying large sums. There is, of course, a degree of arbitrariness in this method but it need not mislead since an itemized list of all expenditures is provided in the Appendix and the reader may make deletions at his discretion.

There is still another problem: the published accounts of the Finance Department are not complete and the accounting practices used by the government were altered from time to time. Discussion of these difficulties has been relegated to the Appendix, and we do no more than note the most essential points here. The figures given in Table XII, which show the amount

TABLE XII

CAPITAL INVESTMENT IN GOVERNMENT ENTERPRISE, 1868–81

Dec. 1867–Dec. 1868............................	¥ 276,728
Jan. 1869–Sept. 1869............................	367,620
Oct. 1869-Sept. 1870............................	1,928,277
Oct. 1870–Sept. 1871............................	1,565,542
Oct. 1871–Dec. 1872............................	3,251,443
Jan. 1873–Dec. 1873............................	4,310,240
Jan. 1874–Dec. 1874............................	5,209,129
Jan. 1875–June 1875............................	1,740,417
July 1875–June 1876............................	3,434,138
July 1876–June 1877............................	3,149,792
July 1877–June 1878*...........................	1,370,016
July 1878–June 1879*...........................	1,409,576
July 1879–June 1880............................	2,933,586
July 1880–June 1881............................	3,706,957
Total	¥34,653,461

* The sharp reduction of industrial investment in 1877–79 was probably the result of the enormous outlay made in these years in suppressing the Satsuma Rebellion.
See Appendix for a discussion of the compilation of these figures.

invested each year between 1868 and 1880 in government enterprises, cover *all* government enterprises after 1876; for the years before 1877 the figures cover only those enterprises under the jurisdiction of the Department of Industry (Kōbushō). Thus, sums invested in such enterprises as the Yokosuka shipyard under the Navy Department, the Tokyo and Osaka arsenals under the War Department, and the Tomioka silk-reeling mill under the Interior Department are not included in the figures for the years before 1877. Since these were all relatively large enterprises, the annual totals for the first nine years shown in the table are substantially less than the sums invested in *all* government enterprises during this time.

On the most conservative estimate, then, the government invested something over 34,653,461 yen, or approximately 5½ percent of its *ordinary revenue*, in government enterprises between 1868 and 1881. As to whether this sum represented the most the government was able to invest in this period we have no way of knowing until we consider the character of competing claims on government revenue. For while the government was establishing industrial enterprises it was also founding technical, medical, and language schools; it was opening consulates abroad, supporting students in foreign colleges and universities, and colonizing Hokkaidō; it was bringing new land under cultivation, expanding and equipping military and naval forces, and improving harbors and rivers. And while the government was building a new order, it was at the same time liquidating the old one, at almost as great a cost.

One of the reasons the transfer of power to the Meiji government in 1868 became permanent was that the new government paid compensation for rather than confiscated outright certain rights and privileges held under the old regime. However happy this strategy of change may have been in other respects, it was not so financially. The new government was saddled with a very heavy financial burden that was in the nature of a fixed charge on income: this burden, once taken up, could be neither thrown off nor substantially reduced without grave political risk. There were three main kinds of expenditure the government assumed in liquidating the old regime. (1) Until 1876, as noted previously, *samurai* and *daimyō* were paid annual rice stipends, and after that date these stipends were commuted at a fixed rate into interest-bearing bonds maturing in twenty years. (2) The government repaid in specie the foreign debts of the *Bakufu* and *han*; a part of the huge domestic debt these governments had accumulated was canceled and the balance was paid in government bonds.[3] (3) Finally, it was necessary to liquidate the old regime militarily. Armed *samurai* rebellions were endemic for ten years after the Restoration, despite efforts of the government to allay *samurai* discontent with rice stipends and pension bonds. How serious a financial strain these rebellions imposed on the government is attested by the fact that in the decade after 1868 the government spent no less than 54 million yen (the equivalent of one year's revenue) in suppressing them.[4]

These three kinds of expenditure took nearly half of the government's ordinary revenue in the years 1868–76.[5] It is impossible to say whether this ratio continued through the period 1876–81 because there is considerable difficulty and uncertainty in distinguishing expenditures belonging to this class in the accounts after 1875. But we may be sure that the cost of liquidating the old regime continued to be a heavy drain on government income since the Satsuma Rebellion came in this period; and it was only in the expenditure of what remained from ordinary revenue after deduction of these first charges on income that the government had any real option. The magnitude and importance of industrial investment can best be assessed in terms

---

[3] The entire foreign debt of the *Bakufu* and *han*, amounting to over 5 million yen, was repaid by 1875; domestic debts of these governments, amounting to upwards of 23 million yen, were assumed by the Meiji government. Ōkuma Shigenobu, "A General View of Financial Policy During Thirteen Years," *The Currency of Japan*, p. 65.

[4] *Mzks*, IV, 20, 372.

[5] See Table XIII.

of this balance. To appraise capital investment in industry in these terms, it will be necessary to limit consideration to the eight years before 1876 because of the ambiguities of accounts after that date.

The ten largest items of government expenditure listed in the accounts for the period 1868–76 are shown in Table XIII. The first four items represent

TABLE XIII
Largest Items of Government Expenditure, December 1867–June 1875

Ordinary revenue for period.............................		¥282,870,871
"Fixed charges"		
Rice stipends	¥95,250,804	
War of restoration and suppression of rebellions.......................	12,940,947	
Repayment of *Bakufu* and *han* debts....	14,949,886	
Money grants for return of rice stipends*	11,699,511	
		134,841,148
Balance of ordinary revenue.............................		¥148,029,723
Army and navy...		47,820,674
Grants from central government to prefectures...............		21,481,385
Capital investment in government industries.................		18,649,396
Loans for encouragement of production.....................		15,388,510
Construction and repair of dikes, roads, and bridges...........		7,623,134
Stipends of officials......................................		5,308,166

* In 1873 the government commuted *samurai* pensions at a fixed rate into a single cash payment upon request. The figure shown in the table represents the total amount of money paid out under this voluntary commutation scheme.

Source: *Mzks*, IV, 20–22.

expenditures that belong to the class discussed above. After these had been subtracted, there remained from ordinary revenue 148,029,723 yen. Capital investment in government enterprises during these years—which, it will be recalled, means only enterprises under the Kōbushō—amounted to upwards of 18 million yen, or just under 13 percent of this balance. (Actual investment was perhaps twice this figure.) The relative significance of this figure stands out clearly in the table. It will be seen that only two items of expenditure exceeded industrial investment, after the deduction of the first four items. The larger of these, the total expenditures on the army and the navy, affords a particularly suggestive comparison.

Not only did *samurai* uprisings in this period contribute to heavy military and naval expenditures, but recent demonstrations of Japan's impotence in the face of foreign pressure gave the nation's leaders a lesson they never forgot in the relevance of force to diplomacy. It must be remembered, too, that expenditure on armaments in this period was abnormally large because the government was creating an entirely new military system rather than expanding an existing one. Suggestive of the importance attached to the industrial program is the fact that capital investment in government enterprises amounted to more than one-third of the sum spent on the army and navy together. Moreover, approximately this ratio was maintained in the years 1876–81. As Table XIV shows, with the exception of two years, 1878

TABLE XIV

INDUSTRIAL INVESTMENT AND MILITARY AND NAVAL EXPENDITURES
(JULY 1875–JUNE 1881)

	Capital Investment in		
	Government Industrial Enterprises	Army	Navy
1875............	¥3,334,138	¥6,959,735	¥2,825,943
1876............	3,149,792	6,904,828	3,424,997
1877............	1,370,016	6,035,940	3,167,512
1878............	1,409,576	6,409,004	2,804,020
1879............	2,933,586	7,766,919	3,079,859
1880............	3,706,957	8,434,529	3,165,222

Source: *Mzks*, IV, 176, 218, 312, 316, 453, 458, 572, 578; V, 14–15.

and 1879, investment in government enterprises amounted annually to a bit more than naval expenditures and a bit less than half of military expenditures, or to nearly one-third of what was spent on the army and navy combined.

It is unnecessary to make other comparisons. The data shown in Table XIII are sufficient to suggest the intensity of the government's effort to develop modern industry. Indeed, when we consider the other claims on government income, it is difficult to see how the government could have invested more than it did in industrial enterprises. Theoretically, investment might have been increased by expanding income, but practically this was impossible, as we shall see.

II

Throughout the first decade or so that it held power, the Meiji government was sorely beset by financial difficulties. As a new and revolutionary government, it had no accumulated reserves to finance the reform program upon which its success ultimately depended. Between December 1867 and December 1868, the first year of power, it was obliged to borrow over 29 million yen to meet expenditures totaling just over 33 million yen.[6] There was no hint of exaggeration in a report of the Financial Affairs Bureau (Kaikei jimu kyoku) in 1868: "The finances of this bureau exist in name only. In

[6] Revenue from taxation in this year amounted to only 3,664,000 yen; extraordinary revenue totaling 29,424,000 yen came chiefly from the following sources: 24,037,000 from the issuance of inconvertible notes; 3,838,000 yen from forced loans (*goyōkin*); and 894,000 yen from foreign loans. Honjō Eijirō (ed.), *Meiji ishin keizai shi kenkyū (Studies of the Economic History of the Restoration)* (Tokyo, 1930), pp. 389–90.

reality our coffers are empty, and our sole function is to negotiate loans. Even day-to-day requirements are met with great difficulty."[7]

Less than three years after this report was written, work was beginning on the Tokyo-Yokohama Railway, the shipyard at Yokosuka was being expanded, and a telegraph line was being constructed half the length of the country to link Tokyo and Nagasaki. How was the capital for such undertakings raised, while at the same time an army and navy were being developed and the old regime liquidated at great cost? If this question can be answered, some light will have been thrown upon the circumstances that permitted Japan to enter directly on industrialization without passing through the intermediate stage of a commercial revolution such as prepared the way in England.

The annual revenue (*sainyū*) of the government in this period was divided by the Finance Department into two categories corresponding to the two major sources from which it was derived. Ordinary revenue (*keijō sainyū*) came from taxation and customs receipts; extraordinary revenue (*rinji sainyū*) came from borrowing and other exceptional measures. These categories will first be examined separately and then in relation to one another.

It is not surprising, in view of the importance of agriculture in the Tokugawa period, to discover that the ordinary revenue of the government in the period 1868–81 came preponderantly from the land tax. Although there are no reliable employment statistics for these years, it is likely that between 70 and 75 percent of the population was employed in agriculture as a primary occupation.[8] As yet there was no significant industrial population since handicrafts were still the dominant form of industrial production and were carried on, for the most part, in peasant households as an adjunct to agriculture. The nonagricultural population consisted of people who rendered services of some kind—government officials, merchants, clerks, innkeepers, doctors, artists, scholars, teachers, priests. Generally speaking, these people were not engaged directly in production, and what they paid in taxes came indirectly from agriculture. The dictum of the Tokugawa writers that agriculture was the basis of the economy still held true, and it was constantly reiterated in official documents of the early Meiji period. It is no wonder this opinion was stoutly held when we compare the revenue yielded by the land tax with total ordinary revenue. Table XV shows these comparative data by years for the period 1868–81.

There is evidence enough to support the conclusion that the yield from the land tax in the early Meiji period was about the same as in the last years of the Tokugawa period. An exact comparison is impossible, but it is safe to say that, if the yield fell off after the Restoration at all, it was only temporarily,

---

[7] *Ibid.*, p. 416.

[8] The earliest government employment statistics (1888) show 71.23 percent of all families engaged in agriculture. Since rural families were then, as now, larger than urban families, the agricultural population was somewhat greater in relation to total population than this figure suggests. *Daishichi tōkei nenkan* (*Seventh Annual Statistical Yearbook*) (Tokyo, 1888), pp. 76–77.

TABLE XV
Annual Ordinary Revenue and Land Tax, 1868–81

	Ordinary Revenue	Land Tax
Dec. 1867–Dec. 1868...........	¥ 3,664,780	¥ 2,009,013
Jan. 1869–Sept. 1869...........	4,666,055	3,355,963
Oct. 1869–Sept. 1870...........	10,043,627	8,218,969
Oct. 1870–Sept. 1871...........	15,340,922	11,340,983
Oct. 1871–Dec. 1872...........	25,522,742	20,051,917
Jan. 1873–Dec. 1873...........	70,561,687	60,604,242
Jan. 1874–Dec. 1874...........	71,090,481	59,412,428
Jan. 1875–June 1875...........	83,080,574	·67,717,946
July 1875–June 1876*...........	69,482,676	50,345,327
July 1876–June 1877...........	55,684,996	43,023,425
July 1877–June 1878...........	49,967,722	39,345,774
July 1878–June 1879...........	53,558,117	40,281,517
July 1879–June 1880...........	57,716,323	41,889,695
July 1880–June 1881...........	58,036,573	42,346,181
Total	¥628,417,275	¥489,943,380

* This figure represents the total revenue for the year 1875–76; the accounts for this fiscal year do not for some reason make the usual distinction between ordinary and extraordinary revenue.

Source: *Mzks*, IV, 48–49, 55–56, 62–63, 68–70, 74–76, 82–84, 90–92, 98–100, 167–70, 193, 263–66, 402–3, 514–18; V, 3, 6.

between 1877 and 1881, when currency depreciation reduced the real value of taxes paid in money.[9] At any rate the income of the Meiji government from the land tax, which accounted for all but 22 percent of ordinary revenue for the period 1868–81, was no greater than the combined revenues of the Tokugawa government and the *han* had been. But the claims upon this revenue were infinitely greater, for the Restoration opened new areas of expenditure without eliminating the old ones.

Extraordinary revenue before 1881 covered the difference between the actual expenditures of the government and ordinary revenue. This difference was considerable. Expenditures between 1868 and 1875, for example, totaled 359,000,000 yen in round figures, while ordinary revenue for the same period came to no more than 282,000,000 yen;[10] and roughly this ratio between outlay and ordinary revenue obtained until 1881.[11] Table XVI indicates the principal means by which annual deficits were met. No less than 73 percent

[9] See below, p. 78.

[10] *Mzks*, IV, 7–8.

[11] The accounts of the Finance Department show that, between July 1, 1876, and July 1, 1880, ordinary revenue amounted to upwards of 274 million yen; extraordinary revenue to nearly 24 million yen. But these accounts do not show all extraordinary revenue. To this should be added 42 million yen borrowed either directly or indirectly (through the issuance of paper money) to defray the cost of operations against Satsuma; and 10 million yen derived from the issuance of Industrial Development Bonds in 1878. *Mzks*, IV, 193–94, 263–66, 401–3, 515–18; V, 3–6.

TABLE XVI
PRINCIPAL SOURCES OF EXTRAORDINARY REVENUE:
DECEMBER 1867–JUNE 1881

A. Extraordinary revenue for period...................... ￥200,298,169

B. Total returns from borrowing and issuance of notes........ 146,585,372

    Issuance of inconvertible notes.......... ￥100,325,444

    Domestic loans

        Goyōkin (forced loans) 5,643,928

        Loan from Fifteenth National Bank.. 15,000,000

        Industrial development bonds 10,000,000

    Foreign loans

        First London loan 4,782,400

        Second London loan 10,833,600

(B equals 73 percent of A.)

Source: *Mzks*, IV, 48–50, 55–58, 62–65, 68–71, 74–77, 83–85, 90–93, 98–101, 167–70, 195–98, 264–82, 402–22, 517–37; V, 3–6, 149–52.

of extraordinary revenue before 1881 came from borrowing (domestic and foreign) and by the issuance of inconvertible notes.

It is clear, then, that the major part of what was classified in the accounts of the Finance Department as "extraordinary revenue" was not revenue at all. No less than 73 percent of it represented debt that had to be repaid eventually from real income. Thus, extraordinary revenue before 1881 was largely future ordinary revenue made available for current expenditure by borrowing. We have already seen how important this class of "revenue" was to the government; and to identify fully the ultimate sources of wealth that supported the program of the Meiji government, it is essential to discover two things. (1) From what future years' ordinary revenue was it drawn? Or, to put it differently, during what years was the indebtedness accumulated between 1868 and 1881 repaid? (2) And from what sources was the ordinary revenue derived during the period of repayment? In approaching these questions, it will be convenient to retain the distinction already noted between indebtedness contracted by direct borrowing and by indirect borrowing through the issuance of notes to be redeemed later.

The first of these categories represents the foreign and domestic loans shown in Table XVI; the principal outstanding on these loans amounted to 38,246,746 yen in December 1880. One column of Table XVII shows the gradual liquidation of this debt between 1880 and 1897; a parallel column indicates the percentage of ordinary revenue derived from the land tax in each year of this period. It will be seen from these data that, by 1892, 59 percent of this debt had been repaid and that the land tax accounted for an average of 58 percent of ordinary revenue between 1880 and 1892. The remaining 41 percent of the debt was repaid between 1892 and 1897, a period in which the land tax averaged 38 percent of ordinary revenue. Clearly it was the expectation of a continuing high rate of income from the land tax that permitted the government, desperately in need of "extraordinary revenue," to

TABLE XVII
Principal Outstanding on Foreign and Domestic Loans, 1880–97

	Principal Outstanding*	Percentage of Ordinary Revenue from Land Tax†
1880	¥38,246,746	73
1881	37,122,986	67
1882	35,958,138	62
1883	30,238,438	57
1884	29,472,322	60
1885	28,775,750	76
1886	28,262,382	61
1887	27,724,504	55
1888	27,150,576	47
1889	26,536,432	51
1890	25,880,320	50
1891	25,178,824	49
1892	13,748,816	46
1893	12,957,280	45
1894	12,110,112	43
1895	9,203,408	40
1896	4,233,752	35
1897	—	30

* Figures represent the amount of debt outstanding on December 31 of each year.
† Figures on the land tax refer to the fiscal year, that is, from June 30 of one year to July 1 of the next.
Source : *Meiji zaisei shi*, VIII, 18 ; Ono Takeo, *Nōson shi*, pp. 50–51 ; *Nihon keizai tōkei sōkan* (*A Synoptic View of Japanese Economic Statistics*) (Tokyo, 1930), pp. 61, 63.

borrow over 46 million yen at home and abroad before 1881 ; and it was the realization of this expectation that enabled the government to liquidate the greater part of this debt between 1881 and 1892 and to meet heavy interest payments on it in the meantime.[12]

The second category of indebtedness was comprised of inconvertible notes, which were outstanding in the amount of 165 million yen in 1878, the peak year.[13] This immense debt was not entirely liquidated for many years,[14]

[12] The conclusion in the text may need clarification. It might be argued that, since the land tax fell from 73 percent of ordinary revenue in 1880 to 50 percent in 1890, it was increased income from other sources that permitted the liquidation of indebtedness in this period. But this argument forgets that if the land tax had not been maintained at the high level it was, increased income from other sources would not have been available for this purpose.

[13] This figure is considerably more than the 100,325,444 yen issued by the government between 1867 and 1881 (see Table XVI). The reason for this is that the figure of 168 million yen outstanding in 1878 includes (1) notes issued by the Meiji government in exchange for notes issued before 1867 by the *Bakufu* and *han*, and (2) notes issued by national banks. The latter are included in the total because they were really proxies for government notes, by which they were secured and into which they were convertible on demand. All figures cited later on the volume of inconvertible paper notes in circulation include bank notes as well as notes issued by the government. *Mzks*, XIII, 466.

[14] Government paper was not entirely redeemed until 1899 ; and the last national

nor was there need to liquidate it completely. Between 1878 and 1886, 47,398,000 yen of these notes were redeemed, and the specie reserve held against the notes that remained outstanding was increased from 4.5 percent in 1880 to 35.7 percent in 1885—from 7,167,000 yen to 42,266,000 yen. As a result, the government was able to make the notes remaining in circulation convertible upon demand as of January 1, 1886; and since by this date the paper yen, which in spite of having been badly depreciated as recently as 1881, was exchanging at very nearly face value for silver in the market, there was no substantial call upon the treasury to convert.[15] The year 1886, then, may be regarded as marking the completion of liquidation of this form of indebtedness.

Of the 47 million yen redeemed between 1878 and 1886, upwards of 12 million were redeemed in bonds, that is, by contracting new debts.[16] In round numbers there remained 35 million yen that were redeemed from ordinary revenue and represented actual repayment of indebtedness. This figure was small by comparison with the original debt of 165 million yen, but the strain of redeeming 35 million yen in a period of seven years may be judged from the fact that ordinary revenue in this period averaged less than 70 million yen annually.[17] And it should be remembered that at the same time the government was increasing specie reserves and making regular payments on the first category of debts. So great an effort required drastic financial measures, especially a heavy increase in taxation. Treatment of this subject will be deferred to a later chapter. It will be sufficient to note here what must be evident from Table XVIII, that the second category of debts, like the first, was repaid primarily through the taxation of agriculture. The period in which this debt was liquidated covers the years 1876–86; and in this period returns from the land tax accounted for an average of 67.75 percent of the ordinary revenue of the government.[18]

III

We return to a question raised earlier: did government investment in industrial enterprises between 1868 and 1880 represent the maximum investment of which the economy was capable? Since, as we have seen, the government could not have channeled a greater proportion of its income into industry than it did, the question reduces to one of whether the government could have increased its income. And, since agriculture represented the only important source of revenue the economy afforded, this is really a way of asking whether the land tax could have been increased.

There are two ways of approaching this question and they tend to complement one another. The first is to compare the Meiji land tax with the tax on

bank note was not retired until 1904. G. C. Allen, *A Short Economic History of Modern Japan, 1867–1937* (London, 1946), p. 46.

[15] Tsuchiya and Okazaki, *Shihon shugi*, pp. 240, 246.

[16] Horie, *Shihon shugi no seiritsu*, p. 177.

[17] *Mzks*, V, 157, 307; VI, 7, 146, 353.

[18] See Table XVII.

TABLE XVIII

	Revenue from Land Tax	Price of Rice*	Volume of Paper in Circulation†
Jan. 1873–Dec. 1873.........	¥60,604,242	¥ 4.80	¥ 79,743,224
Jan. 1874–Dec. 1874.........	59,412,428	7.28	93,897,304
Jan. 1875–June 1875.........	67,717,946	7.28	93,993,817‡
July 1875–June 1876.........	50,345,327	—	100,491,869
July 1876–June 1877.........	43,023,425	5.01	106,891,582
July 1877–June 1878.........	49,967,722	5.55	119,149,843
July 1878–June 1879.........	40,281,517	6.48	166,494,716
July 1879–June 1880.........	41,889,695	8.01	164,354,935
July 1880–June 1881.........	42,346,181	10.84	159,366,836
July 1881–June 1882.........	43,274,031	11.20	153,302,012
July 1882–June 1883.........	43,342,187	8.93	143,754,353
July 1883–June 1884.........	43,537,648	6.26	132,275,012
July 1884–June 1885.........	43,425,996	5.14	124,396,175
July 1885–June 1886.........	43,033,679	6.53	122,153,757

* Average price of rice per *koku* during calendar year.
† Amount of inconvertible notes (including bank notes) in circulation on December 31.
‡ Amount of notes in circulation on June 30.
Source: *Mzks*, IV, 48, 55, 62, 68, 74, 82, 90, 98, 166, 192, 266, 403, 518; V, 6, 160, 310; VI, 10, 150, 357; XI, 46, 699.

agriculture at the end of the Tokugawa period, on the assumption, which seems quite safe, that by the end of the Tokugawa period agriculture was being taxed to the utmost. Second, there are sufficient data available to trace the effects of the Meiji land tax upon the economic position of the peasant and, indirectly, to suggest whether the peasantry could have paid a substantially higher tax.

During the century preceding the Restoration, the Tokugawa and *han* governments fell into serious financial difficulties. The enormous debts these governments bequeathed to the Meiji government bespeak this fact.[19] Increased taxation of agriculture was the easiest and most obvious means of meeting these difficulties, and it was the one most frequently resorted to. As a result, by the end of the Tokugawa period it was not unknown for the lord to take 80 percent of the peasant's crop as land tax although 50 to 60 percent was usual. But regardless of local differences in the rate of taxation, we may be sure that almost everywhere the land tax was as heavy as the peasant could bear. Indeed, there is evidence that in some areas the tax had passed this point and a gradual decline in agricultural population, by famine and flight to the city, had set in.

The Meiji government made no substantial change in the land tax, even locally, until 1873. As it assumed the administration of new areas after 1868, it continued to collect the land tax at the rates in force locally. The govern-

[19] In 1871 the total domestic debt of these governments stood at 68,666,000 yen; 23,345,000 yen of this debt was repaid by the Meiji government; the balance was canceled. Takahashi, *Saikin no nihon keizai shi*, pp. 112–13.

ment had little choice in this matter, for the land tax was too delicate and important to be tampered with in a period as critical as the years immediately after the Restoration. But the Meiji leaders had no desire to perpetuate the old system longer than necessary. Local variations in the rate of taxation were repugnant to the unifying nationalist spirit of the new regime, and an even more serious objection was that the tax was paid nearly everywhere in *kind*, as a *fixed percentage* of the crop. This mode of assessment and payment made the tax cumbersome and expensive to collect, and it made inevitable annual fluctuation in revenue, as harvests varied from good to bad. This in turn made it impossible for the government to plan its expenditures.[20]

These disadvantages led to comprehensive revision of the land tax in July 1873. The old payment in kind was abolished and a money payment established instead. To regularize money income from the tax, the *assessed valuation* of taxable land—which, once fixed, remained constant[21]—was substituted as the basis of taxation for crop yield—which did not. To this same end the rate of taxation remained constant regardless of whether the harvest was good or bad, whereas under the old system it had been necessary to reduce the percentage of the crop taken by the land tax in particularly bad years. It is true the rate of taxation under the new system, originally fixed at 3 percent, was reduced to 2½ percent in 1877, but this reduction was in no way related to crop failure.[22]

The critical step in putting the revised land tax into operation was evaluating taxable land, for obviously it was this factor—once the rate of taxation was given—that determined the weight of the burden placed on the shoulders of the peasant by the new tax. Since the government was borrowing heavily to meet current expenses, it could not afford to suffer any decline in revenue from the land tax. Therefore, the authors of the revised tax consciously established a method of evaluation that would avoid this.[23] The method consisted, in essence, of avoiding market price as the basis of evaluation and arbitrarily placing a value on the total taxable land sufficiently high to guarantee the same total return from the new land tax as from the old. Evaluation was simply a means of commuting a tax in kind into a money tax without loss of revenue by a wholly arbitrary formula designed for the purpose. How effectively this purpose was achieved may be seen from the fact that there was no appreciable difference between the annual average amount of rice that had been collected under the old system and the amount of rice that could be

---

[20] Tsuchiya and Okazaki, *Shihon shugi*, pp. 54–58.

[21] According to the original regulations, taxable land was to be re-evaluated every five years. However, this stipulation was disregarded and, in March 1884, a regulation was issued postponing re-evaluation indefinitely and leaving the original evaluation in force. Katsu Masanori, *Nihon zaisei kaikaku shi* (*A History of Changes in Japanese Taxation*) (Tokyo, 1938), pp. 17, 20.

[22] The new land tax represented an increase over the old land tax *in some districts*, resulting in outbreaks of violence among the peasantry between 1873 and 1877. It was to put an end to these outbreaks that the land tax was reduced to 2½ percent in 1877. Tsuchiya and Okazaki, *Shihon shugi*, p. 49.

[23] *Mzks*, V, 360.

bought at market prices with the money income from the new tax in the first year of its operation.[24]

The prime objective of revision had been to stabilize government revenue. Thus the new tax was based on two constants—assessed valuation and the rate of taxation—in order to yield the same money income year after year. There remained, however, one variable that affected real income from the land tax. This was the price of rice (taken as a convenient index to commodity prices generally), which caused real income from the land tax, as distinct from money income, to vary sharply within short periods. Under the revised system, the landowner owed the government a fixed sum of money each year as land tax; in order to meet this obligation, he had to sell a part of his crop for cash. As his money tax remained constant, how large a part of his crop was taken by the land tax in any given year depended on how much he could get for his rice. (The same was, of course, true of other crops as well.) In other words, the money income of the government from the land tax was worth more in terms of commodities in some years than in others. The land tax and the real income of the government were high when the price of rice (and other farm commodities) was low; and the reverse was true when the price of rice was high. Annual variations in the size of the rice crop were reflected in the market, of course. But the most conspicuous factor in the movement of rice prices in this period was government borrowing through the issuance of paper money, a policy that until 1879 expanded the volume of currency in circulation from year to year.

To follow annual variations in the actual level of taxation after 1873, therefore, it is necessary to take into account fluctuations in the price of rice as well as changes in the rate of taxation. Table XVIII provides the necessary data to follow these two factors between 1873 and 1885. Column one shows money income from the land tax for each year, thus reflecting directly all changes in the *rate* of taxation. Column two shows the average market price of rice in each of these years; that is, it indicates what the money income from the land was worth in terms of the single most important commodity in the economy. Column three shows the single most important factor influencing the price of commodities, namely, the volume of paper money in circulation.

It will be seen from the above table that there was no appreciable change in *real* income from the land tax until the year 1876–77. Both money income from the tax and the price of rice remained fairly constant during this time; the price of rice did move upward in 1874–75, but it returned to its original level almost immediately, despite a large increase in the volume of paper in

[24] The land tax was first collected under the new system in 1875. Money income from the tax in that year was worth 11,819,102 *koku* of rice at current prices. Compare this figure with the yield in kind of the tax in preceding years: 12,549,000 *koku* in 1871; 11,239,000 in 1873; 17,145,000 in 1874. It should be remembered in using these figures that, under the new tax system, the prefectural governments were allowed to collect land taxes up to one-third (one-fifth after 1877) of the amount collected by the central government. Ōno Takeo, *Nōson shi* (*A History of the Agricultural Village*) (Tokyo, 1941), pp. 49–50.

circulation. It would appear that, although the government was borrowing heavily in these years by issuing paper money, the amount of paper in circulation did not outrun the expanding needs of the economy for money. At any rate, there was no marked depreciation of government notes until 1878.[25]

In that year depreciation set in heavily, and there was a corresponding rise in the price of rice. As column three shows, the inflationary movement was the result of the enormous issue of inconvertible notes in 1878–79, most of which (42 million yen) was to defray the cost of military operations against the Satsuma rebels.[26] The volume of paper was reduced somewhat after 1878, but a sufficiently inflationary impetus had already been imparted to carry the price of rice steadily upward until 1882. Other agricultural prices followed.[27] The general inflationary movement, of course, meant an actual lightening of the peasant's tax burden and a serious loss of revenue for the government. The loss was the more acutely felt since the land tax had been reduced from 3 percent to 2½ percent in 1877. Money income from the land tax had been reduced from 50,345,000 yen in 1875–76 to 41,889,000 in 1880–81, while the value of paper money, in which the tax was paid, depreciated steadily between these two dates.

Almost the exact reverse of this movement may be seen between 1881 and 1885. It was in this period that Matsukata Masayoshi, an advocate of deflation, was appointed Finance Minister and succeeded in preparing the way for beginning the conversion of paper money on January 1, 1886.[28] Largely as a result of Matsukata's efforts, the amount of paper in circulation fell from 166,494,000 yen in December 1878 to 122,153,000 yen in December 1885. With each withdrawal of paper after 1881, the notes remaining in circulation took on additional value, and the price of rice declined. That the land tax was *actually* increased by this process may be seen from the fact that money income from the land tax remained remarkably steady in this period of falling prices. In other words, the same tax was being paid in money that was worth more each year. To express this increase more concretely, the peasant was obliged to sell 42 percent more of his crop to pay his land tax in 1885 than in 1881, assuming that his crop was the same in both years and calculating its money value at Tokyo prices.[29]

Although it is not possible with the data shown in Table XVIII to draw an actual graph representing the proportion of the peasant's crop taken by the land tax each year between 1873 and 1886 (we would have to have data

[25] *Mzks*, XI, 205.

[26] Ōkuma, *op. cit.*, p. 64.

[27] *Mzks*, XI, 353.

[28] For a convenient summary of Matsukata's currency reform, see Horie, *Shihon shugi no seiritsu*, pp. 177 ff.

[29] That the production of rice did not increase for the country as a whole in this period may be seen from the following figures: 31,359,000 *koku* in 1880; 29,971,000 in 1881; 30,692,000 in 1882; 30,671,000 in 1883; 26,349,000 in 1884; 34,158,000 in 1885; 27,191,000 in 1886. In the same period the population increased from 35,929,000 to 38,507,-000. *Mzks*, XI, 699.

on total agricultural production and all our data would have to be for uniform periods), we can visualize the general contour of such a graph if we assume an unchanging agricultural yield. The graph line would move irregularly but on the whole horizontally across the graph until 1876–77, when it would dip sharply to reflect the reduction of the land tax from 3 to 2½ percent. Between 1877 and December 1881, a four-and-a-half-year period, the line would move steadily downward, revealing an actual reduction of the land tax due to rising prices. During the following four and a half years, December 1881 to June 1886, the line would return to the 1877 level, very nearly at the same angle of inclination at which it had declined in the previous period.

Our imaginary graph describes fluctuations in the burden on the peasantry imposed by the land tax (assuming a constant agricultural yield) in relation to what it had been in 1873. As we have seen, the 1873 base was the result of commuting the Tokugawa land tax into a money payment, without loss of income or reduction of the actual rate of taxation; and there is reason to believe that the rate of taxation at the end of the Tokugawa period had reached the highest level commensurate with the maintenance of the existing level of agricultural output. If our imaginary graph assesses the relevant factors properly, it is safe to say that the actual rate of taxation in the period 1873–85 never exceeded the rate at which it had been set in 1873, and that in some years (1877–81) it was substantially less. Nevertheless, the land tax took an average of 34 percent of the entire produce of agriculture in this period, according to the estimate of Professor Tsuchiya.[30] But, whether this estimate is accurate or not, there can be no doubt that the land tax already placed an excessive burden on the peasantry and could not have been safely increased, as a survey of the economic position of the peasant in the years immediately after 1880 will show.

IV

In considering the position of the peasantry in these years, it is important to bear the three following points in mind: (1) that the actual, as distinct from the money, land tax became progressively heavier between 1882 and 1885, (2) that it stood by 1885 at approximately the same level as in 1878, and (3) that, even so, it was lighter at the beginning of 1878 than it had been at any time since 1873. It seems fair to infer, then, that the peasantry were not significantly better off, if they were better off at all, during the decade before 1880 than they were in the years immediately following.

There can be no doubt that the position of the peasant was deteriorating rapidly during the first half of the 'eighties. One index of this is the sale of agricultural land for nonpayment of taxes. Paul Mayet, a German economist employed by the Japanese government at this time, states that 367,744 holders lost their land for nonpayment of taxes between 1883 and 1890.[31] Since the earliest occupational statistics show a total of 3,121,075 independent holders

---

[30] Tsuchiya and Okazaki, *Shihon shugi*, p. 60.
[31] Mayet's data are cited from Ōno, *op. cit.*, p. 168.

in 1888,[32] something of the order of 11 percent of all peasant proprietors were dispossessed for nonpayment of taxes in a seven-year period. This, of course, tells but part of the story of agrarian distress. It is probable that only in exceptional cases was land surrendered for back taxes; ordinarily a peasant would borrow, even at the ruinous rates prevailing in rural districts, before letting his land go to the state for a small part of its value,[33] and it seems all but certain that more land was taken by foreclosure than was sold for taxes.

Mayet is the source for other revealing data. He quotes the findings of a series of government surveys of tenancy. According to Mayet, the proportion of arable land worked by tenants in eighteen prefectures rose from 34 percent in 1883 to 39 percent in 1887, and from 39 percent to 42 percent in sixteen other prefectures during the same period.[34] The trend these figures reveal is confirmed by changes in the number of persons qualified to vote and of persons qualified to be candidates in the election of prefectural assemblies. Suffrage was limited to persons who paid a land tax of not less than five yen; in other words, to persons *owning* (tenants did not pay a land tax) land valued at 200 yen or more; and the right of candidacy was limited to persons paying a land tax of not less than ten yen—that is, *owning* land valued at 400 yen or more. The total number of persons in all prefectures who enjoyed suffrage only, declined from 846,258 in 1884 to 722,072 in 1886, a decline of 14 percent in two years. Those who had the right both to vote and to stand as candidates declined from 871,762 to 809,880, or 7 percent, in the same period.[35] It is significant that the number of smaller landowners was declining more rapidly than that of the larger, and it seems reasonable to assume that the decline was even more rapid among the class of landowners who did not hold enough land to vote.

The *Kōgyō iken* paints a dreary picture of the condition of agriculture at this time. Almost everywhere, the study found, conditions were worse than they had been, and almost everywhere this was blamed on falling agricultural prices, which reflected a hidden increase in the actual rate of taxation, as we have seen. A few examples of the findings of the *Kōgyō iken* will illustrate the trend in rural areas and show that it was nation-wide.

One-third of the arable land of Aichi Prefecture was mortgaged, according to the *Kōgyō iken*, and the debt outstanding on mortgages had increased from 1,010,000 yen in 1877 to 4,019,000 yen in 1881, a four-year period dur-

---

[32] *Daishichi tōkei nenkan*, pp. 76–77.

[33] The total taxes in arrears for the 367,744 cases cited by Mayet were 114,178 yen, an average of 31 yen each! This figure becomes credible in the light of the harsh regulations by which the government enforced the collection of the land tax. A regulation of the Finance Department of June 1874 stipulated that the land tax was due on May 15 of each year, that one-half percent interest *per month* would be charged for taxes outstanding after that date, and that land upon which taxes had not been paid in full by August 1 would be subject to forced sale. An amendment of January 1876 reduced the period of grace before forced sale to one full month after the date upon which payment fell due. *Mzks*, VIII, 176–78; Ōno, *op. cit.*, p. 168.

[34] Ōno, *op. cit.*, p. 76.

[35] *Ibid.*

ing which agricultural prices had been on the rise. The total indebtedness on land in Okayama Prefecture was estimated at 7,077,000 yen, an increase of something more than 50 percent since 1879. Ishikawa Prefecture had been hard hit by the decline in agricultural prices since 1881; perhaps 50 percent of the farming land of the prefecture had been mortgaged since then and there was no hope that the bulk of this land would ever be freed of debt. The situation in Tottori Prefecture was similar. The peasants had squandered their income in "idle and luxurious living" when agricultural prices were high, and they now had no resources to carry them through a deflationary period; about half of the land in the prefecture was already mortgaged and the amount of mortgaged land was still on the rise. And so it went through other prefectures. Between 10 and 20 percent of the land was mortgaged in Tokushima, 50 percent in Miyazaki, 30 percent in Nagano, 50 percent in Osaka and Kyoto.[36]

Behind the statistics of agrarian distress lay the ruin of thousands of peasant families. Gotō Shōjirō, one of the wealthiest businessmen of this period, described agricultural conditions in 1888 as follows:[37]

Our people [he means the peasantry] are unable to support the burden of taxation. They have been falling into an ever deeper poverty and they have now reached the point where they cannot maintain life. . . . There were 130,000 holders whose land was sold for taxes in 1882; and between 1883 and last year the number has not been less than 100,000 annually. [These figures are far larger than Mayet's.] How many persons may be reckoned to have fallen into the cruelest circumstances as a result? If we count four persons to a family, approximately 400,000 people a year are being deprived of all means of support. . . .

The data we examined earlier seemed to indicate that the Meiji land tax yielded no more but about the same as the Tokugawa land tax, and this was certainly the government's intention. But if there was any considerable difference, it was the Tokugawa tax that yielded more rather than the other way around. Nevertheless the peasantry seems to have been worse off after the new tax was instituted in 1873. This is reflected not only in the confiscation of land for taxes and the growing rate of tenancy, but in some two hundred peasant uprisings recorded for the first decade of the Meiji period—considerably more than for any ten years of the Tokugawa period.[38]

The explanation is probably that the capacity of agriculture to pay taxes declined somewhat between 1870 and 1885. Foreign trade was undermining a broad sector of Japanese handicrafts that competed with imported manufactures, and the land settlement that accompanied revision of the land tax in 1873 deprived many villages of much or all of their common land and so of a source of free fuel, fertilizer, and building materials. Both of these factors reduced the peasant's ability to pay taxes: the first by reducing his income, and the second by increasing his expenses. Moreover, the Meiji land tax

[36] Ōno, *op. cit.*, pp. 182–84.
[37] Quoted in Kada, *Shakai keizai shisō shi,* pp. 693–94.
[38] Ōno, *op. cit.*, pp. 185–91.

made no allowance for good and bad years as had the Tokugawa tax, and this inflexibility ruined many peasant families in bad years.

All things considered, it seems probable that the Meiji land tax was heavier than the Tokugawa land tax; in any case, it was as heavy as the peasantry could bear. There was never any question of increasing the rate of taxation after 1873, badly as additional revenue was needed; indeed, the only change in the rate of taxation was a downward revision by one-half percent in 1877, in an attempt to stop peasant uprisings by lightening the burden on agriculture. To have increased the tax would have entailed a double risk: of cutting into agricultural productivity by overtaxation and so ultimately reducing government revenue, and of driving the peasantry from rebellion to revolution.

V

Lacking the background of overseas trade, war, and piracy, which created private capital and stimulated private enterprise in the West, Japan was forced to rely on the governmental power to tax and borrow for the financing of industrialization. Despite such limited sources, the Japanese government was able to invest, between 1868 and 1881, something over 34 million yen in industrial enterprises directly owned and operated. Though the amount invested was but 5½ percent of total ordinary revenue, it represented a far greater effort than the figure perhaps suggests; at the same time, the government was pushing modernization on other fronts and liquidating the Tokugawa regime at high cost as well. Only in allocating the remaining half of its ordinary income did the government have any real choice.

At a time when the government was engaged in continuous war with armed *samurai* bands, and the nation was moreover acutely sensitive of military weakness, this same government saw fit to spend nearly 13 percent of the remaining income for investment in industrial enterprises—almost a third of all combined expenditures on army and navy. Since it was loath to borrow abroad, and had little accumulated wealth at home, most of what the government invested in its enterprises came from currently produced surplus—which is to say, from the agricultural sector of the economy. Without an agriculture capable of producing a sizable surplus year after year, the whole Meiji program, including industrial development, would undoubtedly have been impossible. The entire surplus produced by agriculture had to be taken; the peasant had to be relentlessly exploited for the modernization of the non-agricultural sector of the economy. Since this condemned the peasant to poverty and backwardness, it did much to produce the profound gulf between urban and rural worlds that is so obvious and characteristic a feature of modern Japan.

VIII. The Sale of Government Enterprises

THE YEAR 1880 marked the end of the initial phase of Japanese industrialization—in which the government was pre-eminent as promoter, owner, and manager. On November 5 the Dajōkan instructed the departments of the government to sell enterprises under their jurisdiction to private interests.[1] Certain exceptions to the order must have been stipulated later because railways, telegraphs, the Yokosuka shipyard, and arsenals and ordnance works were permanently retained. Otherwise the order was carried out to the letter, and the government's industrial plants were disposed of just as rapidly as private buyers could be found.

The order of November 5 had far-reaching implications for the character of Japanese economic development. Except for the silk industry, modern industrial development under private enterprise dates from this time, as does a trend toward concentration of economic power that went as far in Japan as anywhere in the world. It is true the plants transferred to private ownership by the government after 1880 were, for the most part, small and inefficient by Western standards. But all were equipped with the most modern machinery, the government had trained a labor force and technicians to operate them, and the heavy initial losses getting them into production were past. Perhaps most important of all, they had no domestic competitors and scarcely any in the entire Far East. These were important advantages and they told in the long run. The handful of purchasers of government enterprises never lost the lead they were given, many of them developing into industrial giants in the twentieth century. Japanese historians are agreed on the general outlines of this picture although much research remains to fill in details. This task lies outside our province; we merely cite the consensus of scholarly opinion to establish, at least in a general way, the importance of the sale of government enterprises. What we are concerned with is the sale itself. Why, after investing so much money and effort in these enterprises, did the government dispose of them? Does this indicate that the experiment with government enterprise was deemed a failure, or were there other reasons for the shift of policy?

There are several interpretations of the sale of government enterprises, and each colors the expounder's views of Japan's subsequent economic development because of the central importance all scholars give the measure; or perhaps the converse is nearer the truth. At any rate, none of these interpretations has been carefully documented, and we shall do well in reaching our conclusions to examine the evidence in support of each.

---

[1] Full text of the order in *Meiji zaisei shi* (*A History of Finance in the Meiji Period*) (Tokyo, 1927), XII, 231–32.

There are three main views to be considered. The first, which we may call the "cabal interpretation," is held in some degree by most Marxist historians. According to it, government enterprises were sold at nominal prices and on the easiest terms to a few wealthy families *with the purpose of effecting an alliance between the government and a small but wealthy capitalist class of merchants and ex-daimyō.* Official corruption played no part in the sales, which had their own reward. By the sales the bureaucracy won powerful support at a time it was much needed, and "key industries" were concentrated in the hands of a few people who were thereby able to bring the entire economy under their control and so under indirect government control.[2]

The second interpretation is more subtle. It sees a causal relationship between the rise of political parties and the transfer of government enterprises.[3] Since the Restoration, the argument runs, dissatisfied warriors had been in a state of armed rebellion against the government; beaten decisively in 1877, their opposition did not disappear but took a new and more dangerous form—the political party. To appeal to rural industrialists, who resented heavy taxation and the preferential treatment of city merchants, the *samurai* adopted not only the organizational techniques of Western political parties but their slogans as well. Laissez faire, civil rights, a national parliament, and a written constitution were demanded in the name of progress, civilization, national unity, and international respectability. So effective was this new opposition that the government was driven to make concessions as well as adopt repressive measures. Politically, the opposition was mollified by an imperial rescript of October 12, 1881, promising the nation a constitution by 1889; economically, it was appeased by announcement of the government's intention to dispose of its industrial holdings as rapidly as possible to private purchasers.

A third interpretation holds that government enterprises were sold for financial reasons. The Meiji government, it is pointed out, had by 1880 been living beyond its means for thirteen years, supplementing income by borrowing abroad and by issuing paper money. By 1880 it had become clear that only the most drastic retrenchment would save the government from financial collapse. In December of that year the government held just over 7 million yen in specie against 159,366,000 yen in outstanding notes, and paper money was exchanging at about half face-value for silver.[4] This cut severely into government revenue since the land tax was paid in paper money; trade was disrupted by fluctuating currency values; investment was discouraged, and there was violent criticism of the government both at home and abroad.[5] To

[2] Kobayashi Yoshimasa, *Meiji ishin ni okeru shōkōgyō no sho henkaku (Commercial and Industrial Changes During the Meiji Restoration)* (Tokyo, 1932), p. 26.

[3] The influence of the political parties is nowhere, to my knowledge, emphasized as the primary factor in the sale of government enterprises; but it is often treated as a prominent secondary factor. Horie Yasuzō, *Nihon shihon shugi no seiritsu*, p. 269; and Takahashi, *Meiji taishō sangyō*, p. 147.

[4] Tsuchiya and Okazaki, *Shihon shugi*, p. 240. *Mzks*, XI, 215–16.

[5] To get some idea of the hostility of this criticism, one need only leaf through *The*

save the situation the government embarked on a program of retrenchment and deflation. Students were recalled from abroad and foreign employees dismissed to reduce foreign payments; new taxes were enacted and old ones were increased; government expenditures, including those on armaments, were cut drastically, to produce an annual surplus for purchasing specie and withdrawing paper from circulation. The sale of government enterprises was part of this program. Not only were the usual annual deficits of these enterprises eliminated by sale, but at least a part of the original investment in them was recovered and the considerable operating capital assigned to them was returned to the treasury.

I

Considerable circumstantial evidence can be gathered in support of the "cabal interpretation." For example, no one would deny that, by comparison with the capital invested in them, government enterprises were sold at bargain prices; nor would anyone deny that the buyers were people with excellent government connections. Table XIX summarizes the available evidence of this kind. A number of enterprises have been omitted for lack of data, but the list is sufficiently representative to establish the point that the government took huge losses on the sales. There is evidence, too, that the buyers were men with official influence, as the very list of their names suggests. At one point in an unusually frank autobiography, Takenouchi Tsuna tells of his role in the purchase of the Takashima coal mine by Gotō Shōjirō. To understand fully the significance of his account, it helps to know something of Takenouchi's career. After serving briefly under Ito Hirobumi in the Finance Department, Takenouchi left the government in February 1874 to become a business associate of Gotō. As a businessman he was extremely successful. In time he became a director of several large companies and had a leading part in the construction of a railway from Pusan to Seoul. Family connections and business success brought him political influence. He was elected a member of the first Diet, he served as a trusted mediator between the government and the political parties during the 'nineties, and he was given an important diplomatic mission to Korea on the eve of the first Sino-Japanese War.[6] Takenouchi's account of the Takashima episode is short and to the point.[7]

In July 1874 the *Kōbu taisuke* [assistant to the head of the Department of Industry] went to Nagasaki where he purchased [on behalf of the government] the Takashima mine from an Englishman. Then he returned to the capital. I learned from Ito Hirobumi [under whom the author had served in the Finance Department as late as February 1874] that the prospects of the Takashima mine were excellent and that the government would sell the mine if there were a suitable purchaser. At my urging, Gotō decided to buy the mine. He and I questioned engineers of the Department of Industry and, having made absolutely

Currency of Japan: A Reprint of Articles, Letters, and Official Reports (Yokohama, 1882).

[6] "Takenouchi jijoden" ("The Autobiography of Takenouchi"), *Meiji bunka zenshū,* XXII, 430, 436, 444–46, 448–50.   [7] *Ibid.,* p. 437.

certain of the future of the mine, we decided to request its sale to us. Gotō submitted a petition to the Finance Department on September 20, and permission for the sale was granted November 7.

Gotō was not buying a pig in a poke. The Takashima mine was an already established enterprise and it was the most important coal mine in Japan at the time. The British Admiralty regarded the coal produced there as the best in Asia, and Takashima coal was being shipped to Yokohama, China, and Vladivostok, in addition to supplying the Pacific mail steamers and foreign men-of-war putting in at Nagasaki.[8] And yet this mine was sold to a favored buyer, without competitive bidding. Other enterprises must have been disposed of in the same way; indeed, it is generally acknowledged by historians that the purchasers of government enterprises almost without exception were insiders linked to important men in the government through friendship and family ties.

Up to this point, then, the "cabal interpretation" is convincing. The trouble is that the interpretation is pure speculation beyond this point; it requires us to accept what was undoubtedly a result of the sale of government enterprises, the enrichment of a favored few, *as the reason for the sales*; and there is no evidence at all to prove this. But neither can this inference be disproved: the most that can be said is that the published documents on the subject and the writings of Meiji leaders betray no such intention as the interpretation demands. Other reasons are given for the sales, but there is no suggestion of a desire to benefit a powerful few and win their support for the government. If there was a cabal, it has been extraordinarily well concealed.

The bargain prices and easy terms of the sales—upon which this interpretation places great stress—were less favorable to the buyers than they seem at first glance. In view either of what the government had invested in these enterprises or the profits they subsequently earned, they were disposed of at giveaway prices. But this is hardly a fair way of judging whether the government got enough for them. Assuming for the moment that the government was obliged to sell them, the relevant factor was not what they had cost or would later earn but what the government could get for them at the time. The government had established these enterprises in the first place largely because they could not be financed privately. Private capital was still too weakly developed in 1880 to take them over except at prices amounting to huge subsidies and with long terms of payment. It must be remembered, too, that most government enterprises were not earning profits at the time of their sale;[9]

[8] *Commercial Reports: 1873*, p. 84; also the *Reports* for 1875, p. 67, and for 1882, p. 38.

[9] Although the financial records of government enterprises have not been published, the unprofitability of these enterprises is so frequently referred to in contemporary documents as to leave little doubt on the subject. See Matsukata's remarks in a financial report to the Prime Minister in 1890, "Shihei seiri shimatsu kaidai" ("Report on the Currency Reorganization"), *Mzks*, XI, 215–16; also a petition from the Department of Industry to the Dajōkan in December 1882, *ibid.*, XVII, 305.

TABLE XIX

PURCHASERS AND PRICES OF GOVERNMENT ENTERPRISES

Enterprise	Date of Sale	Government Investment[a]	Purchase Price	Terms of Sale	Purchaser
Fukugawa cement factory..	1884	¥ 169,631	¥ 61,700[b]	25 annual installments[b]	Asano Sōichirō[b]
Kosaka mine	1884	547,476	273,000[c]	¥200,000 in 25 annual installments; balance in 16 annual installments[c]	Kuhara Shōzaburō[c]
Shinagawa glass factory...	1885	189,631	80,000[d]	55 annual payments beginning in 1890[d]	Nishimura Katsuzō[d]
Ani mine	1885	1,606,271	337,000[e]	¥10,000 down; ¥87,000 in 10 annual installments; balance in 24 annual installments[e]	Furukawa Ichibe[e]
Sakai cotton-spinning mill.	1878	———	25,000[f]	15 annual installments[f]	Hamazaki[g]
Okuzu mine	1879	149,546	27,131[h]	¥12,784 in 15 annual installments; balance within 3-year period[h]	Okuda Hamba[h]
Tomioka silk-reeling mill..	———	———	———	———	Mitsui[i]
Fukugawa white brick factory	1884	93,276	83,862[j]		Asano Sōichirō[j]
Takashima coal mine	1874	———	550,000[k]	¥200,000 down; balance in 7 annual installments at 6 percent interest[k]	Gotō Shōjirō[k]

Annai mine	1884	¥675,093	¥ 75,000[l]	¥2,500 down; balance in 29 annual installments[l]	Furukawa Ichibe[l]
Nakaōsaka mine	1884	73,803	25,000[m]	¥250 down; balance in 20 annual installments[m]	Sakamoto Yahachi[m]
Nagasaki shipyard........	1884	628,767	459,000[n]	25 annual installments[n]	Iwasaki Yatarō[n]
Aburato mine	1884	48,608	27,943[o]	¥3,000 down; ¥6,943 within one year; balance in 13 annual installments[o]	————

[a] *Mzks*, XVII, 434–35.
[b] Takahashi, *Meiji taishō sangyō hattatsu shi*, p. 157.
[c] Tsuchiya and Okazaki, *Nihon shihon shugi hattatsu shi gaisetsu*, p. 261.
[d] *Ibid.*
[e] *Ibid.*, p. 260.
[f] *Ibid.*, p. 268.
[g] Kinugawa, *Hompō menshi bōseki shi*, I, 170.
[h] *Mzks*, XVII, 141.
[i] Yokoi, *Nihon kōgyō shi*, p. 152.
[j] *Mzks*, XVII, 309–10.
[k] *Ibid.*, p. 119.
[l] *Ibid.*, p. 132.
[m] *Ibid.*, p. 140.
[n] *Hisho ruisan jitsugyō kōgyō shiryō*, pp. 298–303.
[o] *Mzks*, XVII, 143.

this was, as we shall see, one of the reasons the government wished to get rid of them.

There is evidence that the government at first tried to sell the enterprises on stiffer terms than it eventually got, and failed. In December 1882 the Manufacturing Bureau of the Department of Industry petitioned the Dajōkan to relax regulations governing the sale of government enterprises, complaining that few purchasers could be found under the existing regulations because the down payments and annual installments required were too large; and it asked that the Bureau be given some measure of administrative latitude in these matters. The petition was not acted on until October 1884 when the Dajōkan granted "responsible persons" authority to fix the purchase price and terms of sale for government enterprises, subject only to approval in each case by the Dajōkan.[10] It is significant that, although the Dajōkan, in November 1880, had given the departments of the government authority to sell the enterprises under their jurisdiction, most government enterprises were not sold until 1884. This suggests that not until terms were relaxed did government enterprises generally become marketable.

II

It is extraordinarily difficult to assess the view that the sale of government enterprises was in part a concession to liberal opinion. That public opinion was at times sufficiently strong to influence government policy is true, of course. The imperial rescript of 1881 promising the nation a constitution is an indication of how far the government was forced to go at times to silence criticism. It is at least possible that the sale of government enterprises was a similar concession. But the analogy with the constitutional issue needs supporting evidence; for whereas constitutional government was undoubtedly the central demand of the opposition, there is no evidence that the question of government in business was an issue at all.

It is true that the doctrine of laissez faire enjoyed an extravagant vogue among intellectuals during the decade following the Restoration. During the middle 'eighties, as Japanese intellectuals turned increasingly conservative, a competing school of economic theorists, under the inspiration of German writers, particularly Friedrich List, became dominant. But the earliest guides to economic theory were the writings of English economists—Adam Smith, John Stuart Mill, and Jeremy Bentham. The reasons for this are obvious: Japan and England were both small island countries, and since England was at once the richest and strongest of the Western powers, Japanese intellectuals hoped to find in the writings of Englishmen a secret to the wealth of nations.[11]

---

10 *Mzks*, XVIII, 305. The Nakaōsaka mine provides an example of the difficulty the government sometimes encountered in finding purchasers. The mine was advertised for sale in February 1882 at 67,196 yen; it was not sold until July 1884, when the price was reduced to 25,000 yen, with only 250 yen down (!) and twenty years to pay the balance. *Ibid.*, p. 140.

11 Honjō Eijirō, "Meiji zenki no keizai shisō" ("Economic Thought in the Early Meiji Period"), *Kzskk*, XVII (May 1941), 2.

Fukuzawa Yukichi introduced the ideas of Adam Smith in outline in the second volume of his *Seiyō jijō,* undoubtedly one of the most important books published in Japan in modern times. Other writers either followed Fukuzawa's lead or like him had the naïve hope of finding a universally applicable formula for national greatness in English economic writings. At any rate most of the early writers on economic subjects—Nishi Amane, Tsuda Masamichi, Kanda Takahira, Katō Hiroyuki, to mention the most important— espoused the teachings of English economists.[12]

It is interesting that this school flourished in the years when government policy was most strongly paternalistic, which suggests that theorists had little influence on statesmen. The tariff issue is an extreme example of the incongruity of theory and practice; and it shows, too, how the former was eventually brought into conformance with the latter. While the overriding aim of Japanese foreign policy was revision of the treaties negotiated in 1858 and the enactment of a protective tariff, writers like Taguchi Ukichi were adamantly insisting on the benefits of free trade. But as the 'seventies drew to a close, many of the staunchest advocates of English economic doctrine began questioning the practicability of applying it to Japan. It was becoming apparent that the commercial treaties by which the West had gratuitously foisted free trade on Japan were not at all blessings in disguise. Untrammeled foreign trade was destroying Japanese handicrafts, blocking Japan's industrial development, draining away the nation's supply of precious metals. Recognition that these were undesirable results of free trade posed a dilemma for theorists that they eventually resolved by conceding that, although free trade was sound in principle, Japan's backward economy required some form of protection for an indefinite period.[13]

A similar retreat was made from other liberal doctrines. In a three-volume work published under the title *Minkan keizai roku* in 1880, Fukuzawa concluded that the free play of selfish interests did not necessarily add up to the public good. He wrote:[14]

There are many large enterprises which may be entrusted to private interests but are more beneficial in the hands of the government. Railways, telegraph, gas and water services, for example, are established for the benefit of the people generally. If these public utilities are surrendered to private interests . . . competition will develop. . . . [and] viewed from the standpoint of the nation, this is exceedingly uneconomic.

Fukuzawa, however, went beyond an admission that government ownership of public utilities might be desirable:[15]

If enterprises requiring a large capital are entrusted to private interests, they will be unable to make a profit. Although such enterprises may not be directly

[12] Kiyohara Sadao, *Meiji shoki bunka shi* (*A Cultural History of the Early Meiji Period*) (Tokyo, 1935), pp. 316–18.
[13] Honjō, "Keizai shisō," p. 13.
[14] *Fukuzawa zenshū* (*The Collected Writings of Fukuzawa*) (Tokyo, 1926), IV, 447.
[15] *Ibid.,* p. 448.

related to the public good, still from considerations of long-range national policy, it is difficult to leave them undeveloped and therefore they should be entrusted to the government.

So it was that even the liberal theorists were retreating from laissez faire doctrine by the time the government decided to sell its enterprises.

It was through the efforts of a handful of translators and popularizers like Fukuzawa that Western ideas were made grist for the political mill. Whether liberal economic doctrines won the same acceptance among oppositionist political leaders as among intellectuals is uncertain. But since *samurai* political leaders imbibed political ideas closely associated in Western thought with liberal economics, we may assume that they were at least familiar with the teachings of Adam Smith and his successors. But it does not follow that the ideas of these men were used politically. The choice of ideological weapons from the Western arsenal by Itagaki and his followers, one can not help feeling, was largely opportunistic and consistency was not necessarily an object.

There were good reasons for using Western political ideas in the struggle against the government. One article of the Imperial Oath of 1868 could be interpreted as a pledge of representative government a power-mad clique had left unfulfilled—a serious and telling charge in Japanese terms. Moreover, the establishment of a national parliament, prescribed and guaranteed by a constitution, was, for the wealthy city merchant and rural industrialist, an obvious means of winning a voice in government. The doctrine of laissez faire, to which the government is supposed to have capitulated in selling government enterprises, had no such partisan political value.

There was no important group to which the doctrine might have appealed. For generations the merchant class had operated and prospered under rigid governmental controls, which were regarded as part of the normal environment of business and thought of as a means of winning subsidies, monopoly rights, and other advantages rather than as trammels on enterprise. It is impossible that the business methods and thinking of the merchant had been so profoundly altered since the Restoration that significant numbers of them now found charm in doctrines of economic freedom. Nor were rural industrialists, who were less wedded to government control, likely to have been converts to the novel English doctrine. Why should they, since the government was doing its paternal best to help them (note the aid it gave to the spinning industry) and government enterprises were mostly in fields in which they were not interested?

There are other grounds as well for discounting the importance of government enterprise as a political issue. If the issue had been important, it should have been reflected in the newspapers and magazines of the time, as were other issues between the government and the opposition. There is no trace of this issue in published materials of this kind. Over four hundred newspaper and magazine articles of the first fifteen years of the Meiji period have been published in the *Meiji bunka zenshū*, covering an extraordinary range of subject matter: women's rights, language reform, the tariff question, the improvement of agriculture, civil rights, the question of a constitution, applied science, and so on.[16] But in the entire collection there is not a single article on the question of government enterprise, either pro or con. The same is true of the fifteen-volume collection of newspapers (*Shimbun shūsei meiji hennen shi*) covering the whole Meiji period.[17] Nor is there any allusion to the question of government enterprise in the platforms, resolutions, and petitions of the political parties,[18] which suggests that government enterprise was not a political issue at all.

It is true that the opposition political parties made deficit financing, in part traceable to costly and for the most part unprofitable government enterprises, a major issue. The demand for a reduction of government spending was no doubt popular with rural landlords who suffered from the heavy tax on land and who comprised an important element of the Liberal party (Jiyutō). But there is no more reason to interpret this as opposition to government enterprise than as a protest against expenditures on armaments or any other major item in the budget.

Whatever influence economic liberalism had upon the sale of government enterprises was less direct than has been asserted. Although by no means converted to the ideas of Adam Smith and his successors, members of the government were not wholly untouched by them. Not that government enterprises were disposed of for the sake of an economic (or political) doctrine; but with other reasons for selling them, it was probably comforting to men in the government to know the measure had important theoretical justification. The following quotation from a document written in March 1882 by Matsukata Masayoshi, then Finance Minister and perhaps the most powerful man in the government at that time, indicates quite clearly that the work of the translators and popularizers of the English economists had not passed by him unnoticed.[19]

The natural function of government is chiefly to protect the public interest and guarantee peace to the community. The government should never attempt to compete with the people in industry and commerce. It falls within the sphere of government to look after matters of education, armament, and the police, while matters concerning trade and industry fall outside its sphere. In fact, in these matters the government can never hope to rival in shrewdness, foresight, and enterprise men who are actuated by immediate motives of self-interest.

III

We turn now to the third interpretation, which holds that government enterprises were sold primarily for financial reasons. To judge the adequacy

[16] *Meiji bunka zenshū,* XVII, XVIII.

[17] *Shimbun shūsei meiji hennen shi* (*Meiji History Compiled from Newspapers*) (15 vols.; Tokyo, 1935).

[18] Miyakoshi Shinichirō (ed.), *Nihon kensei kiso shiryō* (*Basic Materials on Japanese Constitutional Government*) (Tokyo, 1939), pp. 173–78, 193–217, 222–30, 234–43, 380–85, 388–400.

[19] Matsukata Masayoshi, *Report on the Adoption of the Gold Standard in Japan* (Tokyo, 1889), p. 54.

of this explanation we need to consider (1) the financial position of the government in 1880, when the decision to sell was made, and (2) evidence that the financial position of the government indeed bore on that decision.

There can be no doubt that in 1880 the government was facing a financial crisis—the product of three closely related factors. We have touched on these factors previously and we need only summarize them here. (*a*) Since the Restoration the government had spent approximately 745 million yen while its income in the same period amounted to only 628 million yen. (*b*) To make up the difference the government had borrowed, chiefly by issuing inconvertible paper money it was pledged to redeem at an unspecified date in the future. (*c*) The willingness of people to accept these notes at their face value steadily declined as the government's specie holdings dwindled. By 1878 the value of paper money began to fall alarmingly, silver went into hiding, the market value of government bonds began to fall, and commodity prices and interest rates began to climb. The government tried various measures to halt the depreciation of paper money, but nothing would avail to sustain its value in the face of continuing loss of specie through foreign trade.[20]

The nature of the crisis the government faced can be described statistically. The first column of Table XX shows the steady depreciation of paper money

TABLE XX

VALUE OF PAPER MONEY AND RELATED PHENOMENA

	Average Value of 1 Gold Yen in Paper Yen	Volume of Paper Notes Outstanding	Specie in Treasury	Ratio of Specie to Paper	Price of Rice* (per *Koku*)
Dec. 1877......	¥1.040	¥119,149,843	¥15,115,405	12.7	¥ 5.55
Dec. 1878......	1.158	165,597,598	17,837,729	10.8	6.48
Dec. 1879......	1.339	164,354,935	9,967,879	6.1	8.01
Dec. 1880......	1.573	159,366,836	7,166,819	4.5	10.84
Dec. 1881......	1.843	154,803,238	—	—	11.24

* Annual average in Tokyo market.
Source: *Mzks,* XI, 244, 278–80, 283, 699.

in relation to gold between 1878 and 1881 ; parallel columns show respectively the volume of currency in circulation, the amount of specie held by the treasury, and the price of rice.

Writing in 1889, Matsukata recalled the alarmed view he took of the swift inflationary movement reflected in the above figures.[21]

At that time [1880] we fell into a condition which filled all classes of the country with anxiety. The real income of the government was reduced by nearly one-half. Among the people, those who lived on interest from government bonds,

[20] *Meiji bunka zenshū,* XVIII, 169.
[21] *Mzks,* XI, 216.

pensions, and other fixed incomes were suddenly reduced to dire straits. Bonds dropped sharply while commodity prices, especially the price of rice, rose to new heights. The land tax was [in reality] sharply reduced, while the value of land appreciated greatly. The farmers, who were the only class to profit from these circumstances, took on luxurious habits, causing a great increase in the consumption of luxury goods. . . . Consequently imports from foreign countries were increased and the nation's specie supply further depleted. Merchants, dazzled by the extreme fluctuations in prices, all aimed at making huge speculative profits and gave no heed to productive undertakings. As a result, interest rates were so high that no one could plan an industrial undertaking that required any considerable capital. All of these phenomena were the result of the temporary creation of purchasing power by the increase in paper money. The deceptive activity in commerce and industry was the result of inflated prices and, in reality, a sign of an accumulating evil. . . . Moreover, the depreciation of paper money revealed the disorganization of our finances to foreign countries and did much to undermine confidence in our government.

By 1880 the supreme objective of the Dajōkan was to restore the value of paper currency, so seriously did the inflationary movement hamper the large policies of the government. If this objective could be achieved, the real income of the government would be restored to parity with its money income, inflationary agricultural profits would be soaked up by what would in effect be an increase in the rate of taxation, and imports would be reduced, the loss of specie arrested, and interest rates reduced to encourage investment. The hardships and dangers the government was prepared to undergo to achieve this object are a measure of the seriousness of the crisis. When Matsukata became Minister of Finance in 1881 to carry out currency reform, he warned the Dajōkan of the difficulties ahead:[22]

I affirmed my conviction that inconvertible paper money was blocking the productive energies of our nation and was the most important cause of the loss of specie. I believed that our most urgent task was to eliminate this evil and restore the value of paper money. [I warned] that, while taking the utmost precautions against the reactions upon the economy that would follow naturally, we must resolutely reform the currency despite all opposition.

The leading members of the government were agreed that drastic steps were necessary to restore the value of currency. But in the discussion of concrete measures a controversy developed that threatened to split the government as disastrously as had the Korean question nearly a decade before. The split developed over a proposal by Ōkuma, a councilor and recently Minister of Finance, to borrow 50 million yen in London for the conversion of outstanding paper notes.[23] Ōkuma's proposal called for a radical departure from past policy, which had restricted foreign borrowing to two small self-liquidating loans. Iwakura expressed the mood of the opposition when he remarked of Ōkuma's proposal: "Rather than raise a foreign loan at the pres-

---

[22] *Ibid.*, pp. 181–82.
[23] Text of Ōkuma's proposal in *Seigai Inoue kō den*, III, 144–46.

ent time, we would do better to sell Kyushu and Shikoku to a foreign country."[24] The split over this issue was the more dangerous because it followed *han* lines, Satsuma men backing and Chōshū men opposing the measure. The deadlock that developed between the two camps was broken and the disruption of the government avoided only by a decision from the throne. The Emperor's decision was against a foreign loan as too dangerous; it killed Ōkuma's proposal and very nearly ruined his career.[25]

Having defeated Ōkuma's proposal, the opposition brought forward one of its own. This was embodied in a long "Financial Memorandum" submitted by Inoue Kaoru to the Dajōkan on August 16, 1880,[26] outlining in general terms the program that was actually followed. Among the steps recommended was the sale of government enterprises. As the Inoue memorandum provides the only direct evidence on the origin of this measure, we will note its contents at some length.

The memorandum began by placing the blame for Japan's adverse balance of trade squarely on government spending. If purchases abroad of equipment for the army and navy, and material, and machinery, and services for government enterprises were eliminated, "the annual difference between exports and imports would be negligible; it is even possible that there would be an excess of exports." Recognition of this fact was essential, for only by reducing imports and building up specie reserves could the value of paper money be restored. There were three means of increasing specie reserves: mining, foreign loans, and foreign trade; but the first two methods were not feasible. Nature had been niggardly and no great increase in the output of precious metals could be expected; and the Emperor had already decided against a foreign loan.

Inoue recommended four measures for maximizing the intake and minimizing the loss of specie through foreign trade. (1) The government should establish a bank, to be called the Bank of Japan, to promote exports by making loans on easy terms to exporters. These loans, moreover, would draw specie into the treasury, for the loans would be made in paper and repaid in specie, after the exporter had disposed of his goods abroad. (2) The government should sponsor the establishment of insurance companies to eliminate payment of insurance charges to foreign companies. (3) The government should also sponsor the establishment of at least ten companies to engage in exporting Japanese goods abroad, thus eliminating the costly services of foreign merchants as middlemen. (4) The government should buy rice on the domestic market with paper money and ship it abroad where payment for it would be received in specie.

To carry this program into effect would require an annual investment of approximately ten million yen. The greater part of this immense sum could be raised by a combination of three measures. (1) Two million yen ear-

---

[24] Text of Ōkuma's proposal in *Seigai Inoue kō den*, III, 149–50.
[25] *Ibid.*, pp. 146–47, 150–51.
[26] Text of memorandum in *ibid.*, pp. 162–73.

marked annually for withdrawing paper notes from circulation could be applied to the program. (2) Taxes on rice wine and tobacco could be raised to yield an additional four million yen a year. (3) Retrenchment of government expenditures could yield another two million yen a year. The memorandum explained the last measure as follows:

Railways, lighthouses, telegraphs, ships, and the like are of course elements of national wealth; also such enterprises as mint money or manufactured iron, silk, paper, woolens, and glass represent progress. If we were to abolish these enterprises, we would be piling loss on loss and nothing would be gained. Consequently, enterprises established by the government should be gradually and in so far as possible sold to private buyers. In addition, we might either shorten the period of service for conscripts or reduce for the next five years the standing army. We might also consolidate and eliminate administrative departments despite the inconvenience this may entail. If we do all these things, we will be able to save at least 2,000,000 yen a year.

After Itō Hirobumi had won the approval of the Ōkuma faction to this program, the government quickly enacted the legislation to carry it out. The limitation on prefectural taxes was raised from one-fifth to one-third of the land tax collected by the central government; grants from the treasury for the repair and construction of prefectural buildings, roads, dikes, and waterways were abolished; the tax on rice wine was doubled and other existing excise taxes were increased and new ones created. On November 5, 1880, the Dajōkan issued identical orders to the six departments of the government, demanding retrenchment. The following order to the Interior Department clearly indicates the reasons for retrenchment:[27]

The present financial reform [requires that] we eliminate unnecessary administrative work and in so far as possible postpone new enterprises (*shin-jigyō*) and eliminate or simplify already existing enterprises and those now being started, thereby effecting a reduction of expenditures by the various departments of the government.

On the same day this order was issued, the Dajōkan issued another, entitled "Regulations Governing the Sale of Factories." The date of the regulation alone suggests it was intended as a financial measure, and the wording of the regulation bears this out, for it indicated what "enterprises" were referred to in the previous order and how they were to be "reduced." The regulation read as follows:[28]

The various factories (*kōba*) established by the government to encourage industry have been organized and equipped. Since the original plan was for the gov-

[27] *Meiji zaisei shi*, XII, 230.

[28] *Ibid.*, pp. 231–32. The British chargé d'affaires, J. G. Kennedy, provided an interesting bit of testimony on the reasons for this measure. He had been instructed to protest against currency depreciation on behalf of the foreign merchants in Yokohama. In a letter of December 3, 1880, Kennedy reported to the Yokohama Chamber of Commerce that: "Mr. Ōkuma . . . assured me that he had used his utmost efforts to provide a remedy. . . . The government have [now] adopted another system and propose by

ernment to surrender these enterprises as they were developed to private owner-ship, this Department will sell the factories under its jurisdiction according to the regulations stipulated in the annex [to this order].

IV

As we have seen, the available evidence strongly suggests that govern-ment enterprises were sold for financial reasons. The depreciation of paper money was depriving the government of important revenue, augmenting the loss of specie by encouraging imports (or so the government thought), damaging the prestige of the government in the eyes of foreigners at a time when treaty revision was the prime aim of foreign policy, and discouraging private investment in industry. To restore the value of paper money, it was necessary to make it convertible, and this required the accumulation of specie. The government hoped to accumulate specie through foreign trade; and one of the few ways of raising capital to promote exports, as the Inoue memoran-dum shows, was the sale of government enterprises.

If sales were made at bargain prices and on easy terms, it was not to enrich a few well-placed men, but because the government could not get more than it did. Most of the enterprises sold were losing money, and there is evi-dence that the government had difficulty disposing of them even at the prices asked. As the quotation from Takenouchi suggests, it is certain that the better buys went to privileged insiders. And many of the buyers later became dominating figures on the industrial scene. But until there is evidence for believing otherwise, this must be accepted as an adventitious result of the sale of government enterprises, not its object.

Nor is there any reason to believe that government enterprises were sold as a concession to the political parties. It is true that liberal economic doctrines had an extraordinary vogue among intellectuals in the years im-mediately after the Restoration and that Itagaki and his followers made use of closely associated political ideas in their struggle against the government. But neither in principle nor in practice did they attack government enter-prise, probably because no important group in the country at that time felt hurt by it. Instead, the opposition stuck to issues that had political appeal—taxation, foreign policy, constitutional government, and civil rights.

---

strict economies in every department, *by the sale of government industries* . . . and by steadily adding to the specie reserve *to bring paper money to par with silver.*" (Italics added.) *Currency of Japan*, pp. 202–3.

Conclusion

MODERN industry in Japan dates from the late Tokugawa period when, under threat of Western encroachment, the Tokugawa and leading *han* built Western-style shipyards, iron foundries, and arsenals. This beginning was important as a prelude to later and more successful industrial efforts, but had little significance at the time, when it was already too late to turn back expansive commercial nations by adopting their superior military technology; more radical innovations were now called for, to modernize the economy as well as armaments. Since the Tokugawa could not do this without destroying the feudal system they were defending, they failed even to protect the country and shortly forfeited their claim to power.

Failure of the old leadership gave opportunity to new men who seized power in 1867, by a political revolution misleadingly called a "Restoration" then and since. These men, who were fiercely patriotic warriors of low rank, not only threw behind industrialization the full power of the centralized state they had newly created; they swept aside whatever stood in the way of economic development, including the class system of which warriors were the chief beneficiaries. Many old values survived and some were even strengthened, to provide sanction for wrenching and painful changes the nation passed through with startling speed and without faltering; but the technology— institutional and industrial—that marked the transition was new.

If the revolutionary use of political power explains the rapidity of this transition, what explains the political revolution? From what source did impoverished and low-ranking warriors draw strength to seize power in 1867? And what made them more than a clique seeking to settle purely warrior grievances? At a time when class loyalties were generally strong, why did they turn revolutionary at the expense of their own class? I have sought an answer to these puzzling questions primarily in the prior development of commercial agriculture and rural industry. This development threw up a class of rural capitalists who dominated the countryside, and it at last made them rebels against the Tokugawa system with its manifold restrictions on enterprise and bias in favor of tamed guild merchants.

We have shown that many of these peasant leaders supported the Restoration movement with money and even men and arms. What we cannot prove, at the moment anyway, is the significance of this support. Meanwhile, if we may assume that low-ranking warriors could not have overthrown the Tokugawa without support of another class, peasant support would seem to have been decisive. The merchants, the only other class that might have given such support, seem on the whole to have remained aloof: there is no satisfactory evidence of revolutionary activity among merchants generally and good reasons for thinking there was none. Not only were the greatest of them tied

101

by economic interest to the shogunate; *samurai* leaders thought poorly of their promise as revolutionary allies. In a letter to a confederate in 1858, Yoshida Shōin wrote: "In the present situation, we cannot of course count on the *daimyō*; nor are the court aristocrats (*kuge*) to be relied on. This leaves us with the peasants." Yoshida does not even mention the merchants as possible allies; and although he goes on to say that the peasants were impotent by themselves, he adds that they could be of great importance with *samurai* leadership.

Once in power *samurai* leaders met the claims of rural capitalists, not fully, perhaps, but in fair measure. On the whole they succeeded in withholding office and political power from their peasant allies, but only by satisfying them in the economic and social sphere. Whereas the Tokugawa had for more than two centuries shackled economic development and enforced stultifying and hateful class distinctions, the Meiji government took daring and resolute measures to promote enterprise and give free rein to talent— abolishing legal distinctions among classes, establishing universal education, withdrawing restrictions on the cropping and sale of land, declaring free the choice of occupation.

Are these and other revolutionary changes to be explained merely by a desire to create the conditions of military power, granting that this and even territorial expansion were objectives of the Meiji leaders from the beginning? I cannot believe so, for the objectives themselves leave unexplained the means chosen to reach them. The shogunate and *han*, for example, had sought the same ends, but by shoring up the feudal system rather than pulling it down, and there were patriotic men after 1867 who thought the pulling down a mistake. The Meiji leaders did not think so, in part because they had seized power with the help of antifeudal elements in the countryside and reform became an end in itself as well as a means to other ends. Moreover, having violated by rebellion the sanctity of the feudal tie, they could not very well build on it but had to create new institutions with the help of allies whose future like theirs was tied to change. Having once turned their backs on this part of the past, they moved forward in the economic sphere by solving problems—immediate practical problems, such as balancing foreign payments, that had to be solved if they were to stay in power; and as they groped for solutions to these problems, they hammered out an industrial policy that was successful, precisely because it was geared to present needs and not to distant and arbitrary objectives.

In developing modern industry the government had no choice but to act as entrepreneur, financier, and manager. Except in the silk industry, where uniquely favorable conditions prevailed, private capital was too weak, too timid, and too inexperienced to undertake development—even with government aid which was given generously but without initial success. Capital could not be raised privately for such large-scale enterprises as railways and mines, and even in fields where capital requirements were much more modest private investors were intimidated by initial technical and organizational difficulties, and by foreign competition.

The government faced many of these same problems, but always with this difference : so long as government enterprises were economically, socially, or politically useful, it was not essential that they be profitable; and so long as the government was able to absorb losses, there were no managerial and engineering problems that could not eventually be solved. Many and perhaps most of the enterprises of our period operated at a loss, which underlines the importance of the government's role in creating modern Japanese industry. But ready as political leaders were for sacrifices, the government could not indefinitely stand the financial strain of heavily subsidizing the new industry ; for it was simultaneously investing lavishly in related forms of modernization—public education, for example—and liquidating the old regime at great financial cost.

For thirteen years the government succeeded in carrying this triple burden. It did so by borrowing and by taxing agriculture, the country's principal source of wealth, as heavily as possible without destroying it or running prohibitive political risks, thus perpetuating the feudal rate although not the feudal form of taxation. By 1880 the rate of expenditure since the Restoration could no longer be sustained and drastic retrenchment was enforced. Among other measures taken at this time to fend off insolvency, government enterprises (excepting those considered strategic) were sold to private buyers for what they would bring, in most cases but a small part of the government's investment in them. This marks an important change in industrial policy. Thereafter, with few notable exceptions, the government sought to develop industry indirectly, by giving technical guidance and various forms of subsidy to private enterprise—a policy that had failed before but now brought very rapid development.

What did government enterprise accomplish between 1868 and 1880? Quantitatively, not much: a score or so of modern factories, a few mines, a telegraph system, less than a hundred miles of railway. On the other hand, new and difficult ground had been broken : managers and engineers had been developed, a small but growing industrial labor force trained, new markets found; perhaps most important, going enterprises had been developed to serve as a base for further industrial growth.

It may be argued that this growth would have come without government enterprise, and that by far the most important achievement of the first fifteen years of the Meiji period was the creation of an institutional environment favorable to economic development. No one would deny the importance of this achievement, but it is doubtful that it would have brought the rapid development it did after 1880 without the experience, organization, and plant contributed by more than a decade of government enterprise. And the speed of development was crucial; for the traditional economy was already failing fast under the destructive impact of foreign trade, threatening prolonged social and political instability. Had it given way, economic development would almost certainly have been delayed or arrested—with political consequences we may surmise from modern Chinese history.

Appendix

IN ESTIMATING capital investment in government industrial enterprises, the period 1867–81 may be divided into three subperiods, each of which presents special problems. These problems are reflected in the final estimate for each period, making impossible a single, unified list of capital investments for the period. Three separate itemized lists are therefore given below; each corresponds to one of the subperiods, and each is introduced by a brief statement of the special problems of the period covered.

First Period: December 1867 to June 1877

Until the fiscal year 1877, the published accounts of the Finance Department are almost useless in estimating capital investment. Before that date the accounts make no distinction between operating costs and capital investment (railways are the only exception); nor do they differentiate the expenditures on specific enterprises within the same general field. For example, expenditures for all government mines are simply listed as "mining expenses," on telegraphs as "telegraph expenses," and so on. Unsatisfactory as these accounts are, it has been necessary to use them for December 1867–October 1870. For the remainder of the first period, there are more discriminating data. The editors of the *Mzks* have compiled a list of annual capital investments in industries under the Kōbushō (established in 1870) from materials to which they had access but did not publish; despite the limited scope of these figures, they have been used as the basic data for the period between October 1870 and June 1877.[1]

The figures taken from this list appear below as *kōgyōhi*, the term used by the compilers.[2] No itemization of this class of expenditures is given in the *Mzks* and consequently none can be given here; but it must be remembered that the figures cover only industries under the jurisdiction of the Kōbushō, thus dropping the estimate for the first period far below the actual figure.[3] Two items have been added to *kōgyōhi*: (1) one-fourth of the annual interest payments on the London loan of 1870, just over one-quarter of which was invested in industry (railway construction);[4] and (2) the expenses of the Kōbushō, as distinct from the enterprises under its jurisdiction. The Kōbushō was concerned exclusively with the administration of government enterprises; it carried on experimental work, surveying, and technical training on their behalf, and it employed a large staff of foreign employees who were essential to their establishment and operation; most of the expenditures of the Kōbushō were, therefore, indirect investments in the enterprises under its jurisdiction and have been regarded as such.[5] In any case, the aggregates added are not great.

---

1 *Mzks*, XVII, 431–32
2 For a definition of *kōgyōhi*, see pp. 107, 110.
3 Most, but by no means all, government enterprises were under the Kōbushō.
4 The loan was for 4,732,400 yen at 9 percent per annum; 1,464,000 yen were spent on railway construction, the balance for nonindustrial purposes. *Meiji zaisei shi*, VIII, 872–73.
5 For a short account of the organization and activities of the Kōbushō, see *Mzks*, XVII, 5–45.

1. December 1867 to December 1868[6]

Mining expenses	¥ 16,627
Telegraph expenses	3,739
Expenses of iron foundries	256,362
Total	¥ 276,728

2. January 1869 to September 1869[7]

Mining expenses	¥ 131,376
Telegraph expenses	4,273
Expenses of iron foundries	231,971
Total	¥ 367,620

3. October 1869 to September 1870[8]

Railway construction	¥1,561,490
Mining expenses	9,702
Expenses of iron foundries	357,085
Total	¥1,928,277

4. October 1870 to September 1871

Kōgyōhi[9]	¥1,334,457
Kōbushō[10]	121,798
One-fourth interest payment on first London loan[11]	109,287
Total	¥1,565,542

5. October 1871 to December 1872

Kōgyōhi	¥2,432,214
Kōbushō[12]	709,942
One-fourth interest payment on first London loan	109,287
Total	¥3,251,443

6. January 1873 to December 1873

Kōgyōhi	¥3,626,670
Kōbushō[13]	574,283
One-fourth interest payment on first London loan	109,287
Total	¥4,310,240

[6] *Mzks*, IV, 48–54.
[7] *Ibid.*, IV, 55–58.
[8] *Ibid.*, pp. 62–65.
[9] All figures listed as *kōgyōhi* for the first subperiod come from *Mzks*, XVII, 431–32.
[10] *Ibid.*, IV, 69.
[11] *Meiji zaisei shi*, IX, 229.
[12] *Mzks*, IV, 74.
[13] *Ibid.*, p. 82.

7. January 1874 to December 1874

Kōgyōhi	¥4,828,919
Kōbushō[14]	281,851
One-fourth interest payment on first London loan	98,359
Total	¥5,209,129

8. January 1875 to June 1875

Kōgyōhi	¥1,506,801
Kōbushō[15]	146,186
One-fourth interest payment on first London loan	87,430
Total	¥1,740,417

9. July 1875 to June 1876

Kōgyōhi	¥3,130,084
Kōbushō[16]	226,148
One-fourth interest payment on first London loan	77,906
Total	¥3,434,138

10. July 1876 to June 1877

Kōgyōhi	¥2,911,942
Kōbushō[17]	170,405
One-fourth interest payment on first London loan	67,405
Total	¥3,149,792

Second Period: July 1877 to June 1879

With the accounts for the fiscal year 1877, it becomes possible for the first time to separate capital investment in government enterprises from the cost of operating them. An order of the Dajōkan dated July 6, 1877, introduced this distinction into the accounts.[18] The order designated all expenditures made on government enterprises as *sagyōhi*, which it then divided into two categories: *kōgyōhi* and *eigyōhi*. All expenditures prior to the beginning of operations were classified as *kōgyōhi*; all expenditures after that date, *including the purchase of new machinery and the cost of new buildings*, were classified as *eigyōhi*. The single exception to this temporal distinction was the cost of materials for subsequent processing; these costs were classified as *eigyōhi*, regardless of when the materials were purchased.

It is unfortunate that the distinction between *kōgyōhi* and *eigyōhi* was made primarily temporal. Since neither of these categories is itemized in the accounts, any capital investment after a factory was put into operation cannot be extricated from *eigyōhi*. Still, it is reasonable to assume that, in a period when government

---

[14] *Mzks*, IV, 90.

[15] *Ibid.*, p. 99.

[16] Strangely, the accounts for this year do not distinguish between expenses of the Kōbushō and of the enterprises under its jurisdiction; the figure given is an average of the figures for 1874 and 1876.

[17] *Mzks*, IV, 218.

[18] *Meiji zaisei shi*, I, 924–34.

enterprises, as a rule, were being started rather than expanded, *kōgyōhi* covered the greater part of capital investments.

Moreover, it is possible to bring the estimate based on *kōgyōhi* somewhat closer to the actual figure by adding another class of expenditure. By the order of July 1877, each government enterprise was provided with a fixed operating capital (*eigyō shihon*) from the treasury. All expenditures classified as *eigyōhi* were to be met from this fund; withdrawals from the fund were to be repaid at the end of the fiscal year from the income of the enterprise. In the event that income was insufficient, the resulting deficit in the fund was to be made good by an allotment from the treasury.[19] Such deficit grants appear in the accounts as *eigyō shihon ketsugaku tempo*. It seems proper to include this category in estimating total capital investment. Not infrequently such deficits were occasioned by the necessity of defraying the cost of new machinery and plant expansion from operating capital (*eigyō shihon*). And in those cases where the deficits reflected actual losses, rather than capital investments, deficit grants from the treasury amounted to subsidies without which the enterprise in question could not have remained in operation.

The other items of expenditure that have been added to *kōgyōhi* in the following table are either included for obvious reasons or explained in a footnote.

11. July 1877 to June 1878[20]

One-fourth interest payment on first London loan	¥	58,692
Navy Department		
Cost of technical school at Yokosuka shipyard		6,538
Cost of dormitory students at school		3,139
Kōbushō		381,875
Colonization Department (Hokkaidō)		
Industrial experimentation		62,324
Eigyō shihon ketsugaku tempo		
Interior Department		
Shimmachi spinning mill		28,586
Kōbushō		
Miike mine		19,300
Chihaya Maru		1,990
Telegraph Bureau		19,300
Manufacturing Bureau[21]		23,148
Kōgyōhi		
Interior Department		
Senjū woolen mill		131,351
Shimmachi spinning mill		35,796
Number one cotton-spinning mill		17,581
Number two cotton-spinning mill		16,691

[19] *Meiji zaisei shi*, I, 927.

[20] Unless otherwise indicated, all figures are taken from the accounts for this year in *Mzks*, IV, 323–61.

[21] This deficit was due to the expansion of facilities. *Ibid.*, p. 345.

Kōgyōhi (*Continued*)
Finance Department
Mint .... ¥   40,431

Kōbushō
Mining Bureau
 Kamaishi mine 173,948
 Nakaōsaka mine 44,123
Railway Bureau 27,812
Manufacturing Bureau
 Akabane factory 7,636
 Shinagawa glass factory......................... 30,043
 Fukugawa cement factory 6,633
 Nagasaki shipyard 39,209
Telegraph Bureau[22] 193,770

  Total ¥1,370,016

12. July 1878 to June 1879[23]

One-fourth interest payment on first London loan .... ¥   50,961

Navy Department
Cost of technical school at Yokosuka shipyard 4,223
Cost of dormitory students at school................... 2,383

Kōbushō 377,801

Colonization Department
Industrial experimentation 117,084

Eigyō shihon ketsugaku tempo
Interior Department 1,574
Kōbushō: Mining Bureau
 Sado mine 29,224
 Ikuno mine 55,842
Kōbushō: Manufacturing Bureau
 Fukugawa cement factory[24]....................... 4,643
 Hyōgo shipyard[25] 10,011

Kōgyōhi
Interior Department
 Senjū woolen mill 34,051
 Number one cotton-spinning mill 2,061
 Number two cotton-spinning mill 3,593
Finance Department
 Mint 49,988

---

22 *Mzks*, XVII, 444.
23 Unless otherwise indicated, all figures are from *ibid.*, IV, 425–53.
24 Deficit due to the purchase of new machinery. *Ibid.*, p. 488.
25 Deficit due to the purchase of new shipbuilding equipment. *Ibid.*, p. 488.

Kōgyōhi (*Continued*)
War Department
Arsenals[26] ....   —
Navy Department
Yokosuka shipyard ....   ￥   16,493
Kōbushō: Mining Bureau
Kamaishi mine   200,776
Nakaōsaka mine   20,166
Kōbushō: Manufacturing Bureau
Shinagawa glass factory   37,527
Fukugawa white brick factory   7,063
Hyōgo shipyard   14,995
Nagasaki shipyard   56,256
Hiroshima mine   95,220
Kōbushō: Telegraph Bureau   129,049

Kōgyōhi (*Kigyōkin shiben*)[27]
Construction cost of Kyoto-Ōtsu Railway...............   75,169
Cost of new operations at Ani mine   6,751
Cost of new operations at Innai mine...................   4,111
Cost of new operations at Aburato mine   4,561

Total ....   ￥1,409,576

Third Period: July 1879 to June 1881

The accounts for this period completed the separation of capital investments from operating expenses that had been partly effected in 1877. An order of the Dajōkan in October 1879 revised the previous definition of *kōgyōhi* to read as follows (italics added) :[28]

This category includes all items of expenditure [on government enterprise] before operations are begun; that is, expenditures for the construction of the factory and subsidiary buildings, and for the purchase of machinery. Also, *expenditures for the construction of additional buildings and the purchase of additional machinery, in order to expand the enterprise after operations have commenced,* are to be classified as *kōgyōhi.*

Although an adequate definition of capital investment was provided by this order, a new difficulty appears. In the previous period, *kōgyōhi* was defrayed entirely from sources shown in the published accounts of the Finance Department. In the period 1879–81 a part of *kōgyōhi* was defrayed from a domestic loan of 10 million yen, raised in 1878 by the issuance of Industrial Development Bonds;[29] the expenditures from this loan were carried in a special account[30] which has never been published. The editors of the *Mzks* have shown the capital invested from this loan in government enterprises under the Kōbushō, but not in industries under the jurisdiction of other departments. Thus capital investments of the latter

26 No figure is given in the accounts for this item. *Ibid.,* p. 502.
27 Items of expenditure shown under *kigyōkin shiben* were defrayed from the 10 million yen raised in 1878 by the issuance of Industrial Development Bonds.
28 *Meiji zaisei shi,* I, 933.
29 *Mzks,* XVII, 452.
30 *Meiji zaisei shi,* I, 945.

class have not been included in the itemized list below, and the total estimate for the period 1879–81, like those for the two preceding periods, is somewhat less than the actual figure.

13. July 1879 to June 1880[31]

Interest on Industrial Development Bonds	¥ 749,861
One-fourth interest payment on first London loan	39,889

Navy Department
Cost of technical school at Yokosuka shipyard	3,126
Cost of dormitory students at school	780

Kōbushō	399,150

Colonization Department
Industrial experimentation	14,092

Eigyō shihon ketsugaku tempo

Interior Department
Tomioka silk-reeling mill	50,000
Senjū woolen mill	19,368

Kōbushō: Manufacturing Bureau
Akabane factory	2,346
Shinagawa glass factory	34,602
Hyōgo shipyard	947

Colonization Department
Sapporo oil factory	17
Sapporo iron-machine factory	1,332
Sapporo silk-reeling and spinning mill	3,492
Atsubetsu water-wheel factory	297
Kayabe cod liver oil factory	420
Hakodate *suimoku* factory	12,701
Nemuro fish fertilizer factory	659
Bekkai canning factory	5,156
Shana canning factory	2,548
Akkeshi canning factory	839
Telegraphs	1,986

Kōgyōhi

Interior Department
Sanjū woolen mill	39,306
Aichi spinning mill	23,866
Hiroshima spinning mill	2,447
Nombetsu sugar factory	99,741

Finance Department
Construction of sodium carbonate factory	46,933

War Department
Arsenals	290,160

[31] The accounts for this year appear in *Mzks*, IV, 515–631.

Kōgyōhi (*Continued*)

Navy Department

Yokosuka shipyard	￥ 41,945
Gunpowder factory	16,946

Kōbushō

Mining Bureau

Sado mine	52,078
Ikuno mine	7,471
Ani mine	6,270
Miike mine	35,099
Kamaishi mine	240,574
Nakaōsaka mine	9,192
Kōsaka mine	22,994
Railway Bureau	15,539

Manufacturing Bureau

Akabane factory	16,621
Shinagawa glass factory	6,991
Hyōgo shipyard	87,477
Fukugawa cement factory	1,000
Nagasaki shipyard	39,433

Colonization Department

Sapporo wrought-iron works	908
Sapporo iron-machine factory	326
Atsubetsu water-wheel factory	12,895
Hakodate *suimoku* factory	10,417
Akkeshi canning factory	9,828

Kōgyōhi (*Kigyōkin shiben*)[32]

Construction cost of Kyoto-Ōtsu Railway	309,964
Construction cost of Maibara-Tsuruga Railway	36,699
Cost of new operations at Ani mine	61,115
Cost of new operations at Innai mine	42,469
Cost of new operations at Aburato mine	9,379
Cost of surveying Tokyo-Takasaki Railway	1,895
Total	￥2,933,586

14. July 1880 to June 1881[33]

Interest on Industrial Development Bonds	￥ 738,697
One-fourth interest payment on first London loan	32,937

Navy Department

Cost of technical school at Yokosuka shipyard	3,126
Cost of dormitory students	780
Kōbushō	208,315

[32] Figures from *Mzks*, XVII, 454.
[33] The accounts for this year appear in *ibid.*, V, 3–157.

Kōbushō: College of Engineering .... ¥ 139,183

Colonization Department
Industrial experimentation 26,271

Eigyō shihon ketsugaku tempo
Interior Department 1,785
Department of Agriculture and Commerce
    Mombetsu sugar factory 20,498
Kōbushō
    Mining Bureau
        Kamaishi mine 27,572
        Nakaōsaka mine 11,704
    Manufacturing Bureau
        Shinagawa glass factory 21,934
        Hyōgo shipyard 11,959
Colonization Department
    Sapporo carpentry shop 4,873
    Sapporo iron-machine factory 2,110
    Kayabe cod liver oil factory 1,009
    Atsubetsu water-wheel factory 3,516
    Sapporo silk-reeling and weaving factory............ 3,457
    Hakodate *suimoku* factory 18,009
    Telegraphs 12,608
    Bekkai canning factory 2,940
    Shana canning factory 3,574
    Nemuro sawmill 928

Kōgyōhi
Finance Department
    Construction of sodium carbonate factory 3,063
    Installation of additional paper-manufacturing machinery.. 2,400
War Department
    Construction of ammunition factory at
        Tokyo Ordnance Works 65,300
    Construction of gunpowder factory at
        Tokyo Ordnance Works 57,370
Navy Department
    Construction of dock at Yokosuka 106,232
Department of Agriculture and Commerce
    Aichi spinning mill 9,856
    Hiroshima spinning mill 20,562
    Mombetsu sugar factory 129,659
    Senjū woolen mill 18,618
Kōbushō: Mining Bureau
    Sado mine 80,000
    Ikuno mine 51,027
    Kōsaka mine 9,989
    Nakaōsaka mine 322

Kōgyōhi (*Continued*)

Kōbushō (*Continued*)

Kamaishi mine	¥ 251,236
Miike mine	62,561
Kōbushō: Railway Bureau	60,769
Kōbushō: Telegraph Bureau	108,970

Kōbushō: Manufacturing Bureau

Akabane factory	13,200
Shinagawa glass factory	16,042
Hyōgo shipyard	86,692
Nagasaki shipyard	71,103
Kōbushō: oil drilling	14,236

Colonization Department

Sapporo water-wheel factory	1,737
Sapporo carpentry shop	6,254
Sapporo foundry	3,373
Sapporo brewery	14,448
Sapporo grape winery	291
Sapporo net factory	1,766
Sapporo *miso* and *shōyu* factory	1,293
Ishikari canning factory	5,881
Sapporo silk-reeling and weaving mill	2,181
Bekkai water-wheel factory	19,980
Telegraphs	1,683
Bekkai canning factory	14,483
Akkeshi canning factory	5,605
Shana canning factory	279
Nemuro sawmill	2,647
Kayabe cod liver oil factory	1,000

Kōgyōhi (*Kigyōkin shiben*)[34]

Construction costs of Kyoto-Ōtsu Railway	220,162
Construction costs of Maibara-Tsuruga Railway	663,300
Construction costs of Tokyo-Maebashi Railway	1,104
Cost of new operations at Ani mine	93,132
Cost of new operations at Innai mine	80,818
Cost of new operations at Aburato mine	29,548
Total	¥3,706,957

[34] Figures from *Mzks*, XVII, 454.

Bibliography

I. Printed Documents in Japanese

Gendai nihon kōgyō shi shiryō (*Materials on the History of Modern Japanese Industry*). Tsuchiya Takao (ed.). Tokyo, 1949.

Ishin sangyō kensetsu shi shiryō (*Materials on the History of the Establishment of Industry at the Time of the Restoration*). Tsuchiya Takao (ed.). 2 vols. Tokyo, 1944.

Kinsei chihō keizai shiryō (*Historical Materials on Provincial Economy During the Tokugawa Period*). Ōno Takeo (ed.). 10 vols. Tokyo, 1931.

Meiji bunka zenshū (*Collection of Works on Meiji Culture*). Yoshino Sakuzō (ed.). 24 vols. Tokyo, 1928–30.

Meiji zenki zaisei keizai shiryō shūsei (*Collection of Historical Materials on Finance and Economy of the Early Meiji Period*). Tsuchiya Takao and Ōuchi Hyōei (eds.). 21 vols. Tokyo, 1931–36.

Mito han shiryō (*Historical Materials on the Mito Han*). Tokugawa kōshaku ke (ed.). 5 vols. Tokyo, 1916.

Nihon zaisei keizai shiryō (*Historical Materials on Finance and Economy in Japan*). Ōkurashō (ed.). 12 vols. Tokyo, 1922–25.

Shibusawa Eiichi denki shiryō (*Biographical Materials on Shibusawa Eiichi*). Vol. I. Tokyo, 1944.

II. Printed Documents in English

Commercial Relations of the United States: Reports from the Consuls of the United States on the Commerce, Manufactures, etc. of Their Consular Districts. No. 12. October 1881.

Commercial Reports by Her Majesty's Consuls in Japan (*1872–1882*). 11 vols. London, 1873–83.

Cowden, Elliot C. "Report on Silk and Silk Manufactures," *Reports of the United States Commissioners to the Paris Universal Exposition, 1867,* ed. William P. Blake. Vol. VI. Washington, 1868.

Japanese Government Documents. W. W. McLaren, ed. *Transactions of the Asiatic Society of Japan.* Vol. XLII, Pt. I. Tokyo, 1914.

Matsukata Masayoshi. *Report on the Adoption of the Gold Standard.* Tokyo, 1899.

Treaties and Conventions between the Empire of Japan and Other Powers . . . since 1854. Tokyo, 1894.

III. Collected Writings

Fukuzawa zenshū (*The Collected Works of Fukuzawa*). Jiji shimpo (ed.). 10 vols. Tokyo, 1926.

Itō Hirobumi. *Hisho ruisan* (*Classified Collection of Secret Papers*). Hiratsuka Atsushi (ed.). 17 vols. Tokyo, 1934.

Iwakura kō jikki (*A True Record of Prince Iwakura*). Tada Takamon (ed.). 3 vols. Tokyo, 1927.

Ōkubo Toshimichi bunsho (*The Papers of Ōkubo Toshimichi*). Hayakawa Junzaburō (ed.). 10 vols. Tokyo, 1927–29.

IV. Contemporary Newspapers and Magazines

Japan Weekly Mail (Yokohama). April to December, 1870.
The Nautical Magazine and Naval Chronicle for 1859 (London). November 1859.
Shimbun shūsei meiji hennen shi (*A Chronological History of Meiji Compiled from Newspapers*). Nakayama Yasumasa (ed.). 15 vols. Tokyo, 1935.
The Tokio Times. January 1877 to June 1880.

V. Books in Japanese

Fujita Gorō. *Hōken shakai no tenkai katei* (*The Process of Development of Feudal Society*). Tokyo, 1952.
———. *Nihon kindai sangyō no seisei* (*The Rise of Modern Japanese Industry*). Tokyo, 1948.
Fujita Takeo. *Nihon shihon shugi to zaisei* (*Japanese Capitalism and Finance*). 2 vols. Tokyo, 1949.
Furushima Toshio. *Edo jidai no shōhin ryūtsū to kōtsu* (*Communications and Commodity Circulation in the Edo Period*). Tokyo, 1951.
———. *Kinsei ni okeru shōgyō-teki nōgyō no tenkai* (*The Development of Commercial Agriculture in the Tokugawa Period*). Tokyo, 1950.
Hattori Shisō. *Meiji ishin kenkyū* (*A Study of the Meiji Restoration*). Tokyo, 1947.
Hattori Shisō and Shinobu Seizaburō. *Meiji senshoku keizai shi* (*Economic History of Dyeing and Weaving*). Tokyo, 1937.
———. *Nihon manufuakuchua shiron* (*Historical Essays on Manufacturing in Japan*). Tokyo, 1937.
Hirano Yoshitarō. *Nihon shihon shugi shakai no kikō* (*The Mechanism of Capitalist Society in Japan*). Tokyo, 1934.
Hirozawa Kiyoto. *Kinsei minami Shinano noson no kenkyū* (*A Study of Agricultural Villages in Southern Shinano During the Tokugawa Period*). Tokyo, 1951.
Horie Eiichi. *Hōken shakai ni okeru sonzai keitai* (*Modes of Capital in Feudal Society*). Tokyo, 1949.
———. *Kindai sangyō shi kenkyū* (*A Study of the History of Modern Industry*). Tokyo, 1948.
Horie Yasuzō. *Nihon shihon shugi no seiritsu* (*The Formation of Japanese Capitalism*). Osaka, 1939.
———. *Wagakuni kinsei sembai seido* (*The Monopoly Sales System in the Tokugawa Period*). Tokyo, 1933.
Inotani Zenichi. *Meiji ishin keizai shi* (*An Economic History of the Meiji Restoration*). Tokyo, 1928.
Ishii Mitsuru. *Nihon tetsudō sōsetsu shiwa* (*Historical Sketches of the Founding of Japanese Railways*). Tokyo, 1947.
Ishii Takashi. *Bakumatsu bōeki shi no kenkyū* (*A Study of the History of Foreign Trade in the Late Tokugawa Period*). Tokyo, 1944.
Kada Tetsuji. *Meiji shoki shakai keizai shisō shi* (*A History of Economic and Social Thought in the Early Meiji Period*). Tokyo, 1937.
Katsu Masanori. *Nihon zeisei kaikaku shi* (*A History of Changes in Japanese Taxation*). Tokyo, 1938.
Kinugawa Taiichi. *Hompō menshi bōseki shi* (*History of Cotton Spinning in Japan*). 3 vols. Osaka, 1938–39.

Kiyohara Sadao. *Meiji shoki bunka shi* (*A Cultural History of the Early Meiji Period*). Tokyo, 1935.

Kobayashi Ushizaburō and Kitasaki Susumu. *Meiji taishō zaisei shi* (*A History of Finance in the Meiji and Taisho Periods*). 20 vols. Tokyo, 1936–42.

Kobayashi Yoshimasa. *Meiji ishin ni okeru shōkōgyō no sho henkaku* (*Commercial and Industrial Changes During the Meiji Restoration*). Tokyo, 1932.

Meiji zaisei shi (*A History of Finance in the Meiji Period*). Ōkurashō (ed.). 15 vols. Tokyo, 1926–28.

Miyamoto Matajirō. *Kinsei shōgyō keiei no kenkyū* (*A Study of Commercial Management in the Tokugawa Period*). Tokyo, 1948.

———. *Kinsei shōnin ishiki no kenkyū* (*A Study of the Attitudes of Tokugawa Merchants*). Tokyo, 1941.

Nawa Tōichi. *Nihon bōsekigyō no shiteki bunseki* (*A Historical Analysis of the Japanese Spinning Industry*). Tokyo, 1948.

Ono Takeo. *Chiso kaisei shiron* (*A Historical Study on the Reform of the Land Tax*). Tokyo, 1948.

———. *Gōshi seido kenkyū* (*A Study of the Gōshi System*). Tokyo, 1929.

———. *Nōmin keizai shi kenkyū* (*Studies in the Economic History of the Peasantry*). Tokyo, 1924.

———. *Nōson shi* (*History of the Agricultural Village*). Tokyo, 1941.

Osatake Takeshi. *Nihon kensei shi taikō* (*An Outline History of Constitutional Government in Japan*). 2 vols. Tokyo, 1938–39.

Sambei Takakō. *Nihon mengyō hattatsu shi* (*A History of the Development of the Japanese Cotton Industry*). Tokyo, 1941.

———. *Nōka kanai sho kōgyō henkan katei* (*The Process of Change in Some Cottage Industries*). Tokyo, 1944.

Sekiyama Naotarō. *Kensei nihon jinkō no kenkyū* (*A Study of the Japanese Population in the Tokugawa Period*). Tokyo, 1948.

Shinobu Seizaburō. *Kindai nihon sangyō shi josetsu* (*An Introduction to the History of Modern Japanese Industry*). Tokyo, 1942.

Shōji Kichinosuke. *Kawamata chihō habutae kigyō hattatsu shi* (*The Development of Habutae Silk Weaving in the Kawamata District*). Fukushima, 1953.

Tabohashi Kiyoshi. *Kinsei nihon gaikoku kankei shi* (*A History of Japanese Foreign Relations in the Tokugawa Period*). Tokyo, 1930.

Tajiri Tasuku. *Zōi sho kenden* (*Biographies of Sages Given Posthumous Court Rank*). 2 vols. Tokyo, 1927.

Takahashi Kamekichi. *Meiji taishō sangyō hattatsu shi* (*A History of Industrial Development in the Meiji and Taishō Periods*). Tokyo, 1929.

———. *Nihon kōgyō hatten ron* (*A Discussion of the Development of Japanese Industry*). Tokyo, 1936.

———. *Nihon zaibatsu ron* (*A Discussion of the Zaibatsu*). Tokyo, 1938.

———. *Saikin no nihon keizai shi* (*Recent Japanese Economic History*). Tokyo, 1932.

———. *Tokugawa hōken keizai no kenkyū* (*Studies in the Economics of Tokugawa Feudalism*). Tokyo, 1930.

Tetsudō in (ed.). *Hompō tetsudō no shakai oyobi keizai ni oyobaseru eikyō* (*The Influence of Railroads on Japanese Society and Economy*). 4 vols. Tokyo, 1916.

Toya Toshiyuki. *Kinsei nōgyō keiei shiron* (*A Historical Study of Farm Management in the Tokugawa Period*). Tokyo, 1949.

Toyama Shigeki. *Meiji ishin* (*The Meiji Restoration*). Tokyo, 1951.
Tsuchiya Takao. *Ishin keizai shi* (*An Economic History of the Restoration*). Tokyo, 1942.
———. *Meiji zenki keizai shi kenkyū* (*A Study of the Economic History of the Early Meiji Period*). Tokyo, 1944.
———. *Nihon shihon shugi ronshū* (*Essays on Japanese Capitalism*). Tokyo, 1937.
———. *Sangyō shi* (*A History of Industry*). Tokyo, 1944.
Tsuchiya Takao and Okazaki Saburō. *Nihon shihon shugi hattatsu shi gaisetsu* (*An Outline History of Japanese Capitalist Development*). Tokyo, 1937.
Yoshikawa Hidezō. *Meiji ishin shakai keizai shi kenkyū* (*A Study of the Social and Economic History of the Restoration*). Tokyo, 1943.
———. *Shizoku jusan no kenkyū* (*A Study of Government Aid to Samurai*). Tokyo, 1942.

VI. Biographies in Japanese

Iida Tadao. *Iwasaki Yatarō* (*Iwasaki Yatarō*). Tokyo, 1937.
Inoue Kaoru kō denki hensan kai (ed.). *Seigai Inoue kō den* (*Biography of the Impartial Prince Inoue*). 5 vols. Tokyo, 1933–34.
Katsuda Magoya. *Ōkubo Toshimichi den* (*Biography of Ōkubo Toshimichi*). 3 vols. Tokyo, 1921.
Kōda Rohan. *Shibusawa Eiichi den* (*Biography of Shibusawa Eiichi*). Tokyo, 1939.
Ōmachi Keigetsu. *Hakushaku Gotō Shōjirō* (*Count Gotō Shōjirō*). Tokyo, 1914.
Shumba kō tsuijo kai (ed.). *Itō Hirobumi den* (*Biography of Itō Hirobumi*). 3 vols. Tokyo, 1942.
Tsurumi Yusuke. *Gotō Shimpei* (*Gotō Shimpei*). 4 vols. Tokyo, 1937–38.

VII. Articles in Japanese

Emi Hiroshi. "Ikuno kyohei" ("The Armed Rising at Ikuno"), *Nihon shi kenkyū* (*Studies in Japanese History*), No. 20.
Etō Tsuneharu. "Bakumatsu ni okeru Kōchi han no shinseisaku" ("The New Policy of the Kōchi Han in the Late Tokugawa Period"), *Kzskk*, XIV (September 1935), No. 3.
———. "Koyū no mengyō yōshiki mengyō no ishoku" ("The Traditional Cotton Industry in Japan and the Introduction of the Western Cotton Industry"), *Kzskk*, XIX (June 1937), No. 6.
———. "Takashima tankō ni okeru kyūhan bakki no nichiei kyōdō kigyō" ("The Joint Anglo-Japanese Coal Mining Enterprise at Takashima in the Late Tokugawa Period"), *Kzskk*, XIII (February 1935), No. 2.
Fukushima Masao. "Meiji shonen no keizai seisaku to shihon chikuseki no mondai" ("Economic Policy in Early Meiji and the Problem of Capital Accumulation"), *Tōyō bunka* (*Oriental Culture*), June 1952, No. 9.
Hara Heizō. "Tenchū-gumi kyohei shimatsu kō" ("A Note on the Rising of the Tenchū-gumi"), *Tosa shidan* (*Tosa History*), March 1938, No. 62; June 1938, No. 63.
Honjō Eijirō. "Meiji zenki keizai shisō" ("Economic Thought in the Early Meiji Period"), *Kzskk*, XXV (May 1941), No. 5.
———. "Reon Rosshu to bakumatsu no shosei kaikaku" ("Léon Roches and

Reform Policies at the End of the Tokugawa Period"), *Kzskk*, XIII (January 1935), No. 1.

Horie Yasuzō. "Bakumatsu no gunji kōgyō" ("Military Industry at the End of the Tokugawa Period"), *Kzskk*, XIX (May 1938), No. 5.

———. "Nakajima Jihei to Yamaguchi han no yoshiki kōgyō" ("Nakajima Jihei and Western Industry in the Yamaguchi Han"), *Kzrs*, XL (May 1935), No. 5.

———. "Tokugawa jidai no rikujō kōtsū" ("Overland Communications in the Tokugawa Period"), *Kzskk*, LI (February 1934), No. 2.

———. "Waga kuni sangyō kakumei no shiki" ("The Beginnings of the Industrial Revolution in Japan"), *Kzskk*, XLVII (October 1938), No. 4.

———. "Yamaguchi han ni okeru bakumatsu no yōshiki kōgyō" ("Western Industry in the Yamaguchi Han at the End of the Tokugawa Period"), *Kzrs*, XL (January 1935), No. 1.

Ishii Kō. "Bakumatsu kaikō-go ni okeru bōeki dokusen kikō no hōkai" ("The Breakdown of the Mechanism of Foreign Trade Monopoly After the Opening of the Ports"), *Sks*, XI (January 1942), No. 10.

Numata Jirō. "Bansho shirabesho ni tsuite" ("Concerning the Place for the Study of Barbarian Books"), *Rekishi chiri* (*History and Geography*), LXXI (May 1938), No. 5.

Ōtsuka Takematsu. "Fukkoku kōshi Reon Rosshu no seisaku kōdō" ("The Policy of the French Minister, Léon Roches"), *Sz*, XLVI (July 1935), No. 7.

Ōyama Futarō. "Bakumatsu ni okeru yōshiki seitetsu jigyō" ("Western-Style Iron Industry in Japan"), *Kzskk*, XX (August 1938), No. 2.

Shōji Kichinosuke. "Fukushima ken kōgyō hattatsu shi" ("History of the Development of Coal Mining in Fukushima Prefecture"), *Shōgyō ronshū* (*Journal of Commerce*), XIV, No. 1.

Tsuchiya Takao. "Keizai seisaku ka to shite no Ōkubo Toshimichi" ("Ōkubo Toshimichi as a Maker of Economic Policy"), *Chūō koron* (*The Chūō Review*), LX (April 1935), No. 4.

———. "Meiji shoki no bōeki seisaku" ("Foreign Trade Policy in the Early Meiji Period"), *Sz*, VI (February 1937), No. 10.

———. "Nihonmatsu seishi kōba no setsuritsu oyobi sōgyō jijō" ("The Establishment and Early Condition of the Nihonmatsu Silk Mill"), *Keizai gaku ronshū* (*Journal of Economics*), II (February 1934), No. 2.

———. "Ōkubo naikyō jidai no shokusan kōgyō seisaku" ("Economic Policy During Ōkubo's Term as Minister of Interior"), *Keizai gaku ronshū* (*Journal of Economics*), IV (August 1934), No. 9.

———. "Takinogawa Kajima bosekijo no soritsu keiei jijō" ("The Founding and Management of the Kajima Spinning Mill at Takinogawa"), *Keizai gaku ronshū* (*Journal of Economics*), III (October 1933), No. 10.

Tsuge Kō. "Ishin zengo no yōmōgyō" ("The Woolen Industry Before and After the Restoration"), *Kzskk*, XIX (May 1938), No. 5.

Yamamoto Itsuji. "Tomioka seishijo setsuritsu to shoki no jōtai" ("The Establishment and Early Condition of the Tomioka Silk Mill"), *Rgk*, VI (November 1936), No. 11.

Yoshikawa Hidezō. "Hiroshima bōsekijo to Hiroshima menshi bōseki kaisha" ("The Hiroshima Spinning Mill and the Hiroshima Spinning Company"), *Kzskk*, XIX (April 1938), No. 4.

———. "Meiji shonen shitsugyō mondai" ("The Problem of Unemployment in the Early Meiji Period"), *Kzskk*, XIV (August 1935), No. 2.

VIII. Books and Articles in Western Languages

Allen, G. C. *A Short Economic History of Modern Japan.* London, 1946.

Barret, F. *L'Évolution du Capitalisme Japonais.* Vol. I. Paris, 1945.

Bird, Isabella L. *Unbeaten Tracks in Japan. An Account of Travels on Horseback in the Interior.* 2 vols. New York, 1882.

The Currency of Japan: A Reprint of Articles, Letters, and Official Reports . . . Relating to the Currency . . . of the Empire of Japan. Yokohama, 1882.

Dyer, Henry. *Dai Nippon, the Britain of the East: A Study in National Evolution.* London, 1904.

Ike, Nobutaka. *The Beginnings of Political Democracy in Japan.* Baltimore, 1950.

———. "Landownership and Taxation in the Westernization of Japan," *The Journal of Economic History,* VIII (November 1947).

Keene, Donald. *The Japanese Discovery of Europe: Honda Toshiaki and other discoverers, 1720–98.* London, 1952.

Mayet, Paul. *Agricultural Insurance in Organic Connection with Savings Banks, Land Credit, and the Commutation of Debts,* tr. Arthur Lloyd. London, 1893.

Norman, Egerton Herbert. *Japan's Emergence as a Modern State: Political and Economic Problems of the Meiji Period.* New York, 1940.

Ōkuma, Shigenobu (ed.). *Fifty Years of New Japan.* 2 vols. 2d ed. London, 1910.

Paske-Smith, M. *Western Barbarians in Japan and Formosa, 1603–1868.* Kobe, 1930.

Raoulx, Jean. "Les Français au Japon: La création de l'arsenal de Yokosuka," *Revue Maritime,* May 1939.

Sansom, Sir George B. *The Western World and Japan, a study in the interaction of European and Asiatic cultures.* New York, 1949.

Takahashi, H. K. "La place de la Révolution de Meiji dans l'histoire . . . agraire du Japon," *Revue Historique,* CXX (October 1953).

Takizawa, Matsuyo. *The Penetration of Money Economy in Japan.* New York, 1927.

Taniguchi, Kichihiko. "Strukturwandlungen des Japanischen Aussenhandels im Laufe des Industrializierungsprozess," *Weltwirtschaftliches Archiv,* XLVI (1937: II).

IX. Statistics

Daisan tōkei nenkan (Third Yearbook of Statistics). Tokei in (ed.). Tokyo, 1884.

Meiji taishō zaisei shōkan (Finance in the Meiji and Taishō Periods). Toyo keizai shimpo (ed.). Tokyo, 1929.

Nihon bōeki seiran (A Handbook of Japanese Foreign Trade). Toyo keizai shimpo (ed.). Tokyo, 1935.

Tōkyō fu tōkei sho (Statistics on the Tokyo Metropolitan District). Tokyo, 1882.

X. Bibliographies

Honjō Eijirō. *Kaihan nihon keizai shi bunken (Revised Bibliography of Japanese Economic History).* Kyoto, 1933.

———. *Nihon keizai shi daisan bunken (Third Bibliography of Japanese Economic History).* Tokyo, 1953.

Nachod, Oskar. *Bibliographie von Japan, 1906–1912.* 2 vols. Leipzig, 1928.
———. *Bibliographie von Japan, 1927–1929.* Leipzig, 1931.
———. *Bibliographie von Japan, 1930–1932.* Leipzig, 1935.
Praesant, Hans. *Bibliographie von Japan, 1933–35.* Leipzig, 1935.
Tsuchiya Takao and Ōuchi Hyōei. *Meiji zaisei keizai shi bunken (A Bibliography of the Economic and Financial History of the Meiji Period).* Tokyo, 1933.
Wenckstern, Fr. von. *A Bibliography of the Japanese Empire . . . from 1859 to 1893.* Leiden, 1895.
———. *Bibliography of the Japanese Empire . . . from 1894 to the middle of 1906.* Tokyo, 1907.

Index

123

Recent Publications in the Stanford University Series, History, Economics, and Political Science.

SERBIA BETWEEN EAST AND WEST: The Events of 1903–1908. WAYNE S. VUCINICH

"This is a scholarly work of high quality on an important section of modern European history. . . . It is gratifying to see [Dr. Vucinich's] work included among Stanford University publications inaugurated happily in 1922 by R. H. Lutz's penetrating appraisal of the German Revolution 1918/19. Professor Vucinich has put to good use his training in history and his linguistic equipment. He gives us a much-needed story of Serbia as it marched from weakness and chaos toward political consideration and active partnership in Balkan affairs."—*Political Science Quarterly* $4.75

SCIENCE AND RELIGION IN AMERICAN THOUGHT: The Impact of Naturalism. EDWARD A. WHITE

"A significant contribution to a major enterprise—the revival of a specifically Christian interpretation of history . . . an attractive performance; it will stimulate those who have studied this material in other sources. Above all, it has the freshness that can come only from deep sincerity."—*Mississippi Valley Historical Review* $2.50

16